AUTHENTIC
DISCIPLESHIP

A STEP-DRIVEN BIBLICAL PROCESS FOR SPIRITUAL GROWTH

MARTIN HARRIS

ISBN 978-1-64300-895-0 (Paperback)
ISBN 978-1-64300-896-7 (Digital)

Copyright © 2018 Martin Harris
All rights reserved
First Edition

All rights reserved. No part of this publication may be reproduced, distributed, or transmitted in any form or by any means, including photocopying, recording, or other electronic or mechanical methods without the prior written permission of the publisher. For permission requests, solicit the publisher via the address below.

Covenant Books, Inc.
11661 Hwy 707
Murrells Inlet, SC 29576
www.covenantbooks.com

CONTENTS

Preface..7
Chapter 1: The Elemental Component 9
Chapter 2: The Written Law of God 13
    The Nature of the Law..15
    The Law Described 16
    Love Revealed by the Law 19
    The Law as a Teacher of Righteousness..................22
Chapter 3: Vicarious Atonement...................................27
    Atonement through Christ.....................................29
    God's Desire for Reconciliation 32
Chapter 4: The Failure of Human Judgment................36
    The Woman Caught in Adultery............................40
    Pharisaism: A Substitute for True Righteousness....44
    The Revelation of the Human Spirit 46
    Only Righteousness Can Judge Righteousness.......47
    Is the Law the True Righteous Standard? 48
    The Essence of Spiritual Leadership 59
    Loving Leadership Involves Righteous Judgment...63
Chapter 5: The Process of Spiritual Growth 65
Chapter 6: Factors Which Contribute to
                Spiritual Growth 73

Chapter 7: Faith 76
    Faith as Part of Daily Life 78
    Faith Encompasses a Large Part of Our Lives 81
    Shifting Sand 88
    The Good Fight of Faith 91
Chapter 8: Virtue 94
    The Holy Spirit Convicts 96
    Questionable Acts 100
    Carnality in Christianity 102
Chapter 9: Knowledge 105
    The Pursuit of Knowledge 107
    The Nature of Knowledge 109
    The Trustworthy Compass 111
Chapter 10: Self-Control 114
    Prayer is the Answer to the Question 116
    Willpower: Doing the Tough Stuff 121
    Living in a Fallen World 125
    Self-Control and the Power of the Holy Spirit 128
    Dealing with Immorality 133
    An Ounce of Prevention Is Worth a Pound
    of Cure 136
Chapter 11: Perseverance 138
    Our Perseverance as a Reflection
    of His Perseverance 139
    Christian Examples of Perseverance 141
Chapter 12: Godliness 145
    Godliness is Devotion to God 147
    The Enemy of Godliness 149
    Examples of Godliness 151
    Godliness Versus Religion 153

Chapter 13: Brotherly Kindness 156
    Paul's Account of Brotherly Love 160
    Crippled Love 162
Chapter 14: Divine Love 166
    Αγάπη, Divine Love of God the Father 168
    Love, the Only Gift That We Can Give to God...169
    The Supremacy of Love for Ministry 170
    When Divine Love is Imitated.............................172

Conclusion...175
Bibliography..179

PREFACE

The Christian walk is a journey on a road that has two ditches, one on either side parallel to each other. One ditch is self-righteousness, and the other is license. We must stay out of both ditches.

The Lord commands us to live uprightly, separated from the world and hating sin but not preoccupied with it. He charges us to be light and salt in the world. However, mature Christianity does not qualify us to be judges of other's Christian experience, only our own.

The purpose of this book is to teach Christians who want to know how to be worthy of the name. Christian maturity, for many decades, has been subjective. Its determination was based upon the observations and judgment of other's Christian walk. We teach the truth all the while looking for evidence of its presence in our students. Many Evangelical/Fundamental churches tend to judge by appearances. The result is a grade of pass or fail. Sometimes we define our Christianity in terms of personal or organizational qualifications, and the result is alienation of our Lord's servants. As James says, "These things ought not to be so." The church leadership for so long has chosen

Pharisaism as the means of judgment, and as a result, many have been hurt. The Lord tells us that the royal law is to love your neighbor as yourself. This has been commanded from the beginning as the supreme mark of a disciple. The command is located in Leviticus 19:18 and compounded by our Lord in Matthew 22:39.

Christian growth is a process. Peter shows us the steps and the result, and Paul defines it for us. We are to be Christlike. Jesus is Emmanuel, "God with us." He is 100 percent God and 100 percent man. This was established as orthodox by the Council of Chalcedon in AD 451 as quoted by Cairns, "The council held that Christ was 'complete in Godhead and complete in manhood, truly God and truly man,' having 'two natures without confusion, without change, without division, without separation.'"[1]

The authentic process of Christian growth leads to the love that Jesus commanded and asked of Peter. John tells us that our Father's nature is this love that Jesus commanded. Christ is God; God is Love; we are to be Christlike, and when we do, the world sees Jesus Christ through us. They will not see Him physically, but they will see the character of Christ in us. We declare Him with our love and virtue.

---

[1] Earle Edwin Cairns, *Christianity through the Centuries: A History of the Christian Church*, Rev. and enl. ed., 2d ed (Grand Rapids, MI: Zondervan Pub. House, 1981), 136.

• C H A P T E R •
1

The Elemental Component

If you ask the world what love is, the answers vary with every person you ask. Everyone has an opinion, but all of them are subjective. Arguably one of the biggest problems in the world today is the lack of a standard of truth by which we can communicate our thoughts. We have twisted the meanings of words in English so that many are opposite of their original intent. For instance, "cool" means good, and "hot" is good as well. A "dog" is a worldly man and so is a "cat." In another time, "cat" meant a shrewish woman. Of course, it also still means a feline. Other words mean something entirely different from their original word. A "rod" is a car, gun, or cylindrical bar. "Love" is another good example. It can mean deep affection, brotherly kindness, sensuality, or an excuse to be uncooperative (it's for their own good).

Love means one thing to the person who has enjoyed it through personal experience and something else to the victim of abuse. An orphan might define it in terms of security while the children of "at-home parents" might consider it in terms of the discipline, goodwill, and the sacrifice of those who provide for them. Statesmen may define it as patriotism while the revolutionary might say fighting for freedom to deliver from tyranny. In essence, love is defined by the world usually by personal experience.

Real love is the willingness, even desire, to commit personal sacrifice for the benefit of others because they are precious and maybe not even familiar. The world is unable to invoke this kind of love. The reason for this is the difficulty such love presents to basic human nature. Crabb says, "To involve oneself with another for the purpose of ministry is risky. It requires that we concern ourselves with another's welfare rather than our own. Easy words. But vulnerable ministry offered to people who cannot be trusted to respond appreciatively is frightening, and when their response is neglect or rejection, the pain can be unbearable."[2] We all tend to be self-protective. I'm sure it comes from our experiences of selfishness in others that makes it difficult for us to let our guard down. The result is an attitude of fear that tends to resist expressions of selflessness.

My favorite genre of motion picture is the war movie. It's not just the noise and the adventure but the extreme in

---

[2.] Larry Crabb, *Understanding People: Deep Longings for Relationship* (Grand Rapids, MI: Ministry Resources Library, 1987), 197.

human experience and attitude. I see in it the widest range of human emotion which perhaps defines the contradiction that is the spirit of man.

War movies incorporate loyalty and betrayal with the most serious of consequences. We see courage and terror, diligence and sloth, wrath and indignation. We see love in a purer degree and selfishness as well.

And finally, I ponder the great love of God who sent His Only Son to endure the degradation of a sinful world and suffer untold torment in place of the sinners who crucified Him. This is the kind of love of which the world knows nothing: a love so great and so incomprehensible as to drive me to my knees when I think of it. What kind of love would compel a man, who though no crime or sin of His own, to quietly suffer untold torment when miraculous rescue was available with no more than the whispering of a request? What kind of love would drive Him to endure the wickedness and injustice of a world for thirty-three years and in the final moments of the ultimate injustice cry out to the God of Heaven, "Father, forgive them for they know not what they do." No doubt, it is the greatest love ever known. This is what it means to be Christian. Branscomb tells us that in His teaching, Jesus prescribed a different way to accomplish the will of God than the Sadducees and Pharisees of ancient Judah: "As he preached he also taught that the righteousness of that kingdom meant—active love toward God and man. We have seen how he said that love was the central and dominant element in the life of those who would do the will of God."[3]

[3.] B. Harvie Branscomb, *The Message of Jesus* (Nashville, Tenn.: Abingdon-Cokesbury, 1926), 114.

• CHAPTER •

2

THE WRITTEN LAW OF GOD

When God sent His Only Son to earth, He did it to show the depth of His desire to redeem man. His love for us led Him to send His most precious possession for our redemption. Not only did He send Jesus for our salvation but in doing so, He showed us grace. Not just a desire to save us from the penalty required by the law but to extend His care as a father. Undeserved favor, that is Divine Grace. Grace is a quality of the greater person who condescends to the lesser, not with arrogance or haughtiness but with compassion and understanding. Chuck Swindol writes, "On occasion royalty in England will make the news because someone in the nobility will stop, kneel down, and touch or bless a commoner. That is grace."[4] Jesus revealed Himself to sinful men with the purpose of saving from the penalty of the law. which is death. The Father has declared

---

[4.] Charles R. Swindoll, *The Grace Awakening* (Dallas: Word Pub, 1990), 8.

to us His love by sending Jesus the Christ to reveal Himself to us as Savior and Son. Jesus walked the earth as the only completely righteous man. His compassion for suffering sinners yet His unflagging affirmation of the law shows the middle road which must be travelled by those who understand what love is. John tells us,

> And of His fullness we have all received, and grace for grace. For the law was given through Moses, but grace and truth came through Jesus Christ. No one has seen God at any time. The only begotten Son, who is in the bosom of the Father, He has declared Him. (John 1:16–18, NKJV)

The middle of the road without the grace of Jesus Christ is impossible. It cannot be achieved because the penalty of the law allows no acquittal, and the carnal nature of man allows no mercy. Thiessen says, "The universal sinfulness is not limited to acts of sin; it includes also the possession of a sinful nature."[5] There is either complete obedience or total failure with no middle ground possible. The possibility of hope comes through the forgiveness of the penalty (death) which can only be achieved when a person can walk the earth in complete righteousness, having been subjected to

---

[5]. Henry Clarence Thiessen and Vernon D. Doerksen, *Lectures in Systematic Theology*, Rev (Grand Rapids: Eerdmans, 1979), 185.

the same temptations as every man. The law of sin and death has only one judgment, pass or fail. The death of the Savior, however, has provided a second alternative for sinful man.

> For the law of the Spirit of life in Christ Jesus has made me free from the law of sin and death. For what the law could not do in that it was weak through the flesh, God did by sending His own Son in the likeness of sinful flesh, on account of sin: He condemned sin in the flesh, that the righteous requirement of the law might be fulfilled in us who do not walk according to the flesh but according to the Spirit. For those who live according to the flesh set their minds on the things of the flesh, but those who live according to the Spirit, the things of the Spirit. (Romans 8:2–5, NKJV)

The Nature of the Law

But what of the law now? Can it be summarily dismissed? Absolutely not, it must be superseded or fulfilled by something more effective for God's purposes. The law reflects the nature of the Father. Hodge says, "These two principles, then, are to be taken for granted; first, that moral good is good in its own nature, and not because of its tendencies, or because of its conformity to the laws of reason; and, second, that all law has its foundation in the nature and will of God."[6] It can no more be disregarded than the Father Himself. The law is an integral part of who God is and what is characteristic of us being His children. Again, Hodge says, "In other words we do not refer the sense of moral obligation to an externally revealed law, as its source but to the constitution of our nature."[7] So in essence, the law and its penalty is a direct function of the nature of God. The penalty of breaking the law is demanded by God Himself with no other authority. God is the highest judge and executioner. Death is completely the result of the Father's judgment against individual sin. If the law is an integral part of the Father's nature, it must as well be a part of our nature, if we truly are born again. We can no more cast aside the law than we could our own nature.

The Law Described

C. S. Lewis describes the relationship of God to the moral law (the Ten Commandments) very well. He says,

---

[6.] Charles Hodge, *Systematic Theology*, Vol. 3 (Grand Rapids: Eerdmans, 1993), 262.
[7.] Ibid., 266

"The other bit of evidence is that moral law which He has put into our minds. And this is a better bit of evidence than the other because it is inside information. You find out more about God from the moral law than from the universe in general just as you find out more about a man by listening to his conversation than by looking at a house he has built."[8]

Moses brought the Hebrews out of Egypt by the command of the Lord God. He guided them across the Red Sea where the Lord parted the waters. They arrived at Mt. Sinai and waited on the Lord. He ordered Moses to set up a barrier around the base of the mountain and post archers along it to kill any person or thing which attempted to cross.

One thing the law does is to show us our complete separation from God. Moses alone was allowed to cross. He went up Sinai where God wrote the moral law on two stone tablets with His own hand. Moses received all of the commands of God and was instructed to relay the information to the Hebrews. He made them agree to keep the commands of God and sealed the covenant in blood. This is the Old Testament.

---

[8]. C. S. Lewis, *Mere Christianity: A Revised and Enlarged Edition, with a New Introduction, of the Three Books, The Case for Christianity, Christian Behaviour, and Beyond Personality*, Macmillan paperbacks ed (New York: Macmillan Pub. Co, 1984), 37.

Basically, the law breaks into three parts. The first is the ceremonial law, which regulates how God must be approached; second is the moral law, which accedes to the righteous nature of the Father; and finally, the laws of daily life. The laws of daily-life controlled sanitation, litigation, and dietary requirements etc., while the moral law showed right and wrong from God's perspective. Since the ceremonial law primarily sanctified God from sin, when Jesus broke down the wall of separation, it was no longer needed. Paul tells us that the law has been superseded.

> And you, being dead in your trespasses and the uncircumcision of your flesh, He has made alive together with Him, having forgiven you all trespasses, having wiped out the handwriting of requirements that was against us, which was contrary to us. And He has taken it out of the way, having nailed it to the cross. (Colossians 2:13–19, NKJV)

Verses 13 through 14 declare the fulfillment of the moral law. The ceremonial law has been done away with as the writer of Hebrews tells us: "Let us therefore come boldly to the throne of grace, that we may obtain mercy and find grace to help in time of need" (Hebrews 4:16, NKJV). Branscomb gives us insight as he speaks of Jesus and the ceremonial law: "Jesus declared that nothing that went into a man made him unclean, and in that one statement they (Pharisees) clearly recognized that he swept away a great portion of the ceremonial law."[9]

The law of Moses no longer has authority over the Christian. It has been nailed to the cross along with our sins. Where there is no sin, there is no justification for death which is the penalty of the law. The catch, of course, is that as long as we are in the flesh, sin will always be a possibility; however, the penalty no longer applies. The law is now a final reminder of the possibility of sin and allows the Holy Spirit to change behavior through repentance. It can no longer function as punisher of transgressions in the born-again Christian.

Love Revealed by the Law

It is a kind of strange twist to the average person, but God's love is indirectly revealed in His law which also judges and condemns us for our sin. It is difficult to understand, but the severe penalty that is carried by violation of God's law reveals the depth of God's love for us. By showing the magnitude of His righteousness in relation to our own, He has revealed His love in granting to us eternal life. In this way, the law compels us to an understanding of the depth of God's love by showing the depth of God's aversion to sin

---

[9.] B. Harvie Branscomb, *The Message of Jesus* (1926), 40.

and the seriousness of His judgment against it. It is in the violation of the law that we see all the horror, wickedness, and evil in the world. The violation of the law is the cause of all death whether it is from disease, violence, or old age. This is why God can grant eternal life when our sins are completely forgiven. Of course, the body will fail because death is the process that is begun at birth, but the real man lives on. God promises a new body, an eternal one when life in this world is done. "The wages of sin is death" (Rom 3:23, NKJV).

However, in order to understand the depth of God's love, we must understand that the severity of the punishment for sin is extreme from our perspective. But since God is the ultimate judge and His righteousness is supreme, the punishment is just from His point of view. Our point of view has no bearing at all.

In contrast to the supreme, holiness, and goodness of God, we have the unrighteousness of man. His depravity can be seen best through the eyes of God Himself.

In Daniel's visions, the gentile kingdoms are pictured as rabid, vicious animals in the eyes of God. Since Daniel was God's prophet, his dreams reflect the mind of God. The gentile kingdom of Nebuchadnezzar is depicted as a lion. The kingdom of Alexander the Great, as a leopard and a goat, represents the Medo-Persian Empire. The Roman Empire would be depicted as a vicious beast of no earthly origin. The hubris of the unregenerate mind is that earthly power is represented by predatory beasts. Carnal men respect power of life and death and the control of others. It confirms their exalted opinions of themselves.

It is in contrast with the goodness of God's nature that true human depravity is recognized. As a result, even through human eyes, the fact of our "wrongness" is apparent. No one is more wrong or worse than anyone else because all are wicked in comparison to God the Father. When we read "There is none righteous, no not one," we know it's the truth in the depth of our souls.

The book of Romans in the first three chapters reveals to us the depravity of man in all his horror. By depravity, I mean the inability of man to satisfy or accomplish the righteousness acceptable to God by any means or even to know Him at all. The book of Romans teaches us that man in his sinfulness and on his own merit is not worthy of God's consideration at all. How can good people be capable of the Holocaust, the pogroms, the revolution of the Khmer Rouge, the Chinese Communist Revolution, the French Revolution, and the Inquisition and have within them any good at all? Many people today like to think of these mass genocidal horrors as oddities and exception to the general goodness, civility, and nobility of man or even the product of a few isolated, twisted individuals but not all men. But these are only few tiny examples of man's barbarity. The scale of lies, murders, and man-induced suffering of the innocent is even to man himself surprising. Our total depravity is undeniable.

We see that God has made plans to reveal Himself to man (to give man something to compare human unrighteousness to). His revelation first came to persons of His own choosing, but that limited His salvation to only a select few. This is not God's complete plan for man. His desire is to bring every one of us to repentance and salvation abandoning no one. Two Peter 3:9 tells us, "The Lord is not slack concerning His promise, as some count slackness, but is longsuffering toward us, not willing that any should perish but that all should come to repentance" (2 Peter 3:9, NKJV).

He revealed Himself to Israel through the law then to those who came in contact with them. His first revelation to an entire nation of people came through the law. He taught the elements of His righteousness by revealing sin and the complete separation of Himself from that sin through the written and declared law of Moses. He showed His own nature in its opposition to the nature of man.

The Law as a Teacher of Righteousness

John Stott comments, "In our case, too, nothing can convince us of our sinfulness like the lofty, righteous law of

God."[10] The law teaches the righteousness of God in all His purity and the total inability of man to achieve that same righteousness on his own, period. Those who know this best are those who have tried to keep the Law and through honest introspection, recognized their failure. The sad truth is that Christians still have the sinful nature within them and are just as capable as the world to commit sin.

That is the entire purpose of the law—to show us who we really are without any dissimulation or self-delusion. McQuilkin says, "Like the light in the washroom, God's law reveals man's moral defilement (Romans 3:20, 7:7). By the law comes the knowledge of sin. If I do not believe I am dirty, I will not seek cleansing."[11] Of course, this is from God's perspective not from ours. He has no need of "law"; He is righteousness. We, on the other hand, must have a simple standard or canon by which we recognize our true natures, not ultimately for the purpose of correction but true self-identification like a lit vanity mirror in an actor's dressing room. It magnifies our sin and failures in order to bring about recognition and repentance and, of course, "walking worthy of the Gospel." The law strips away our pretense and delusion of self-righteousness by showing us what true righteousness is and telling us we cannot achieve

---

[10]. John R. Stott, *Basic Christianity*, 1st ed (Grand Rapids, Mich: Eerdmans, 1986), 70

[11]. Robertson J McQuilkin, *An Introduction to Biblical Ethics* (Wheaton, Illinois: Tyndale House Publishers, 1989), 51.

it. None may honestly look into the bright countenance of the law and stand. It unilaterally declares and judges us using our own consciences as accuser to be unfit and unworthy. McQuilken says, "Our moral judgment is distorted by our cultural environment and therefore is not an adequate oral light to follow."[12] Even to the most twisted humanity capable of understanding wrong, it screams out the truth. Paul recognized this in Romans 7 where at the end of the chapter, he cried out from the recognition of his own depravity, "O wretched man that I am, who will deliver me from this body of sin?" This realization is the turning point in any Christian's walk with God. The pursuit of holiness now becomes unquestionable, and the path becomes illuminated. It doesn't have to be argued for or defended in any way.

As I read through the Bible, it strikes me that God is so far above me that for Him to give me and all my depravity any kind of consideration at all is unfathomable; yet, He does. But why would God show me the law and then tell me that I can never ever fulfill its righteous demands? It seems terribly unfair to hold a man to a standard that can never be achieved, but God has His reasons. He wants us to know Him, yet He insists upon our recognition of His divine holiness. Doesn't it seem reasonable that He, being the very definition of sinless purity, would necessarily and completely be repulsed by even the purest among us? I think so.

[12.] McQuilkin. *An Introduction to Biblical Ethics* (1989), 55.

I cannot likely know the reasons for God's actions, but it seems to me that absolute perfection in conjunction with absolute authority and power could not tolerate our unrighteousness; else, it would be condoning it. His love would, being of the same magnitude as His perfection (complete and absolute), have to find a way to bridge the gulf if anyone is to be forgiven, accepted, and saved from destruction. But before He could hold us guilty of our unrighteousness, He would have to show us true righteousness so that we would know our responsibility and agree with it. If not, then our destruction would be no better than taking our anger out on a helpless animal. He must reveal to us what true righteousness is in order to be just. Every parent understands that the child has to know what he did wrong before he is punished so as not to repeat it. Declaring to us the law would fulfill such a requirement. By showing us our unworthiness, He would begin the process of revelation that began in the garden and continued on through the birth, ministry, death, and resurrection of Jesus Christ, revealing righteousness without any doubt. The process would culminate with the complete destruction of unrighteousness and all the consequences of it in the apocalyptic, last days. As a result, the law is completely satisfied and just.

But if anyone is to be saved, the consequences of transgression must be dealt with. In this way, the law shows us the value of our salvation, the justice in our punishment, and the incomprehensible grace extended to us in our forgiveness. In short, it reveals God's deep and abiding love. God must reveal our unrighteousness so that when He presents the solution, we can see just how valuable and precious it is. The punishment for sin must be total, but by contrast, the solution must be total as well. Since the law is total, mercy must be total as well.

• CHAPTER •
3

Vicarious Atonement

Vicarious atonement is a theological term which means that atonement or appeasement for a wrong that is made by someone other than the offender. Think of it like a default on a loan which is paid by a cosigner. The person who fails is not held accountable by the lender. The cosigner becomes the burden bearer. I defaulted on the debt of righteousness I owed to the Father, but Jesus bore my burden on Himself in my stead. I can then be forgiven for His sake.

When I am forgiven of my sin and its penalty, then I am no longer held responsible for the violations of my past. But what about tomorrow? Am I perfected such that I will no longer sin? Not a chance. My sinful nature is still present, and I still have all the components that got me into trouble in the first place. The first benefit of atoning vicarious sacrifice is mercy or forgiveness of past error. The second is sanctification or assurance of continued forgiveness of future failure. The same sacrifice is sufficient for past, present, and future. "For by one offering He has perfected forever those who are being sanctified" (Hebrews 10:14, NKJV).

What else can we say about the law? The law is the contract with the lender that I violated. Its judgment went into effect as soon as I sinned the first time. The problem, of course, is that I can never satisfy the contract. I am responsible.

But if I am to be held responsible to the law of sin and death, then what good does it do for me if I can never satisfy it? There must also be a way for me to find hope; otherwise, I would say, "What's the use?" God's love must find a way to prevent discouragement. In other words, sinners must be encouraged with hope, yet the Holiness of God must be satisfied for man to have any kind of a friendly relationship with the Father. Man's frustration is obvious in the vast number of religions which claim intimacy with the God of Heaven based solely upon human effort. Human effort for righteousness cannot save. If it could, the atoning death of the Lord Jesus would have been unnecessary. It would also reveal that human responsibility was even greater because people could simply choose not to do evil. History teaches us, without doubt, that such is not the case. We are incapable of good if left to our own devices.

Of all the belief systems that permeate world religion, the idea of atonement through works seems to be the lowest common denominator. The Buddhist, the Muslim, many pseudo-Christian groups, and Judaism all attempt the salvation that one form of law or another brings. The problem, of course, is that if our salvation is granted based upon our efforts, it is a wage earned and not a gift of grace. "For the wages of sin is death, but the gift of God is eternal life in Christ Jesus our Lord" (Romans 6:23, NKJV). My dad always taught me, "Never thank a man for your paycheck, you earned it."

Paul is clear that "In His (God's) presence no flesh shall stand" (Galatians 2:16, NKJV). This means that I can have no argument before God. There can be no defense for my offenses. No lawyer can plead my acquittal based upon my value earned or intrinsic. Atonement may only be achieved through the grace and the willingness of God. Salvation, then, must be the forgiveness of the penalty of the law of sin and death and the institution of a right relationship with God. This could only come about by atonement for our transgressions against Him. Atonement will be the gateway to the path of forgiveness which ends in salvation because it completely covers over past transgressions by the willing substitution of Christ's life for our life.

Atonement through Christ

We see pretty clearly that no one is acceptable by merit. No one can achieve the quality of righteousness and the forgiveness of past sins that would gain for them God's acceptance by works. Forgiveness should be impossible. Its possibility, however, is provided by love. The forgiveness of God is an outworking of His love.

It is in the atonement that the depth of love that God has for us is revealed because the cost in suffering by His Only Son was so intense, and the satisfaction of the law is so out of our reach.

God has established, without any room for doubt, that only the shedding of blood will satisfy His wrath at sin. God's anger at sin is immense. It requires extreme measures to satisfy.

In ancient Israel, many conditions were necessary for the reception of God's forgiveness. Sacrifice of great personal effort was required, not only in the provision of the blood sacrifice itself but in the depth of the offender's desire for forgiveness.

Such depth would be known by the great efforts necessary to live under the prescripts of the law. Such efforts are pictured in the difficulties and restrictions imposed to enter the Holy Place. As Bruce says, "But our author is thinking of the priestly and sacrificial structure of the earthly sanctuary where everything spoke of the difficulty of approaching the throne room of God. The nearer to that throne room one approached, the more prohibitive were the barriers and the fewer the people who were permitted to pass through them."[13] It would be necessary to travel to the tabernacle or temple in order to offer the blood sacrifices required for sin as we read in Hebrews, "Without the shedding of blood is no remission" (Hebrews 9:22, NKJV). Further, the sacrifices were to be of the very best the offender had to offer making them even more precious.

Hebrew men would walk from all over Israel with their families and provision for many days just to attend the feasts and present the offerings. Such efforts would indicate a great depth of devotion. In those days, God would grant forgiveness to be stored up until the sin question could be resolved in a final and completely satisfying way. Therefore, forgiveness was granted on a conditional basis. God granted forgiveness based on the faith exhibited by the obedience of the penitent and the depth of his contrition compelling him to go to these extreme measures to satisfy the requirements of God's holiness and His law.

But even this devotion in itself was not enough, for as soon as the penitence was made, some other sin would creep in, and the whole process would start all over again. Man would and could never become righteous on his own.

[13.] F. F. Bruce, *The Time Is Fulfilled: Five Aspects of the Fulfilment of the Old Testament in the New*, The Moore College Lectures 1977 (Grand Rapids: Eerdmans, 1978), 86.

God's Desire for Reconciliation

But God wants man close to Him. God knows that by the works of the law, no one can be made righteous since none can keep the law perfectly. The sin nature within precludes it. Neither can one be justified by devotion, effort, or obedience for the same reason. Hypothetically, salvation then becomes dependent upon a man's ability to keep a great depth of devotion continuously in his mind and soul. Continuous perfection is the only acceptable level. But man is still wrong in his nature leading to this same "wrongness" in his mind always lusting to satisfy himself and not God.

As has been said before, if it were possible for man to achieve the righteousness necessary to stand in the presence of God in all His holiness through living by the dictates of the law, the sacrifice and life of Jesus Christ Himself would be unnecessary. We could claim justification by the moral weight of our good against that of our evil. The difficulty with this thinking is the subjective nature of the argument. I may give greater weight to one sin and less to another. Men tend to judge in a subjective way. "I am righteous because I make such an effort to be righteous," he says as he determines stealing to be a greater sin than not loving the Lord with all his mind, soul, and body. The final decision would have to rest with God Himself of course, since He is the One offended.

But since the defendant would determine the weight or efficacy of obedience to a particular standard at the moment of temptation, he could argue for its righteousness. This might leave the condemnation and righteous judgment of the law open to question. If all are guilty even when only the smallest infraction occurs, then there is no argument possible; a defendant would have to argue himself absolutely sinless to be acquitted. Therefore, the arguments of Paul in the book of Romans and the requirement for atonement are proven to be necessary. Since our transgressions are undeniable and unstoppable, forgiveness of sin for all time must be complete and is required if we are to be saved.

Under the law, it is still impossible to achieve righteousness because of past sin and the proclivity to future sin. The only way that righteousness can be achieved is if the sin debt is fully paid, past, present, and future. No remainder or reminder is permissible. Such forgiveness requires a monumental, miraculous, and divine effort. God must satisfy His holiness that is outraged at our sin. His love must provide a means for both His pure nature and His desire to bring man to Him in a familial relationship. Holiness calls for the destruction of the sinner, but love yearns for his life. This is the Divine dilemma. How can forgiveness be given without destroying the veracity of the law and denying the holiness of the Divine Nature? The way chosen by the Father is vicarious atonement. Atonement is the reparation made for offenses; vicarious means "in substitution." Two methods of atonement are mentioned in the Bible. The first is by substitution through grace. This means that God forgives based upon the sacrifice of Jesus Christ who in essence suffers death in the place of every guilty person who would ask for forgiveness in faith. The second is by works.

But what is meant by, "works atonement?" Simply put, the idea is that something I do sacrificially will square me with God. He and I can reach an understanding that allows me to be forgiven. I can make up for my evil by doing good things that I have sacrificed for. I can balance out the scales of righteousness by offering against all my evil the weight of all my good. This is atonement by works, but the Bible teaches that salvation is by grace through faith, not of works eliminating boasting.

It is the hardest thing in the world for people to accept that the gift of grace is without any hope of repayment. People just cannot accept a free gift. They look for means to justify the gift. Perhaps it is reluctance to be obligated. Perhaps it is the need to feel of personal value and, therefore, importance. This is a foolish notion since a supreme being would of necessity be superior in every quality that human beings feel is valuable. How could our works be valuable or redeeming to such a One?

But human nature persists in trying to prove its worth by performing "good deeds" or acts of benevolence or even the supreme sacrifice. Most think that because they perform acts of sacrificial merit (a very subjective judgment), they are progressively made good. In actuality, the reverse is true. The more I justify myself, the more my arrogance and pride grows. Soon I foster the idea that I don't need God; I can save myself. So my "good works" become evil since they progressively lead to perceived self-sufficiency. Once again, hubris takes over. We can be so proud of ourselves. This in itself is the sin that God hates the most.

• CHAPTER •
4

THE FAILURE OF HUMAN JUDGMENT

In 1961, a psychologist at Yale University conducted a series of tests to try and scientifically determine why otherwise normal moral people could commit the horrors of the Holocaust. His question was prompted by the capture, trial, and execution of Adolf Eichmann, the notorious commandant of Auschwitz concentration camp during WWII whose defense was "I was only obeying orders." His findings rocked the academic world. People were selected and paid to administer a series of questions to another person whom they had met but could not see during the test. They could, however, hear the other person. In the event of a wrong answer to the question, the "teacher" was told to administer an ever increasingly painful and dangerous electric shock. Unknown to the teacher, the "learner" was part of the testing staff and only acted a response to the shock which was never really administered. The phony shock was administered by the teacher, and the staff member would scream in pain and beg to stop. The amazing result was that the teacher kept administering the shock even to a lethal level. Of the people who were teachers, only a very few refused. The conclusion was that most people would cooperate with an authority figure even to the extent of lethal torture. When the teacher was asked "Who bears the responsibility for the students' suffering?", the most common answer was "I don't know." The point is that most people tested were capable of torture just because they were told to. Sixty-five percent (two-thirds) of participants (i.e., teachers) continued to the highest level of 450 volts. All the participants continued to 300 volts. Sure, their conscience made them feel guilty, but they did not stop. The depravity of man is evidenced not only by his failure to do good but by his willingness and in some cases, eagerness to do evil. Dr. Milgram concluded that his experiments were indicative of cultural indoctrination, but in 1944 Germany, there was a different culture from America. Milgram's findings have been replicated in a variety of cultures, and most lead to the same conclusions as Milgram's original study and in some cases, see higher obedience rates. Without God and His law, there would be no recognition of evil and means to bring it under control. We would all be at the mercy of the "law of the jungle," and only the strongest would survive.[14]

---

[14]. "Milgram Experiment," *Wikipedia*, December 30, 2017, https://en.wikipedia.org/w/index.php?title=Milgram_experiment&oldid=817773912.

Perfect good must be present before good works are truly good. Hodge says, "In other words, a work is good when there is nothing either in the agent or the act which the law condemns. In this sense, not even the works of the holiest of God's people are good."[15] This means only God is good, and only through Him can works be good. He is the only One who is perfect. He is the only judge. This is why our judgment of good and bad is ineffective and our work of righteousness valueless.

Even mature Christians find themselves judging righteousness by works. "Look at Joe, he goes to church, he doesn't drink or smoke, he only watches the news on TV, he never goes to 'R' movies, he tithes the tenth, he teaches Sunday school, he obeys the laws of the land, he never listens to rock and roll music, he never lies or takes what does not belong to him. Oh, what a Godly man he is!" Do actions make a man "righteous?" If they do, then why did Jesus say, "Woe to you, scribes and Pharisees, hypocrites! For you are like graves which are not seen, and the men who walk over them are not aware of them" (Luke 11:44, NKJV)?

Their outward appearance was by all observable standards "righteous," yet their hearts were far from God. The only conclusion is that righteous acts do not make a man righteous because our hearts are so depraved. Truly righteous acts come only from a truly righteous person. This

---

[15]. Hodge, *Systematic Theology*. Vol. III. 232.

is impossible from a corrupted heart and mind. Studies of behavior have shown a huge number of neuroses and psychoses that affect us and our relationships with others. "The Diagnostic and Statistical Manual of Mental Disorders (DSM) is the American Psychiatric Association's standard reference for psychiatry which includes over 450 different definitions of mental disorders."[16] Just the fact of so many identified mental disorders must say something about the perfection of the human mind, soul, and emotions. If we were so capable of judging what is right, why are we so disturbed? Righteousness for man comes only by God's grace. God's free gift of imputed righteousness (imputed means "deposited to our account") is without works of any kind. But our outward righteousness is suspect, and our judgments of the righteous acts of others must therefore also be faulty. To say it differently, "Appearances can be deceiving."

People love to take satisfaction in their work. "The Preacher" in Ecclesiastes teaches that taking satisfaction in our work is one of the very few things that are not "vanity." Our spiritual acts are sometimes looked upon in the same way. Since I have made such efforts and since they are of such value to me, they must be valuable to God as well. After all, is this not a good measure of my devotion to Him? Our good works then become a substitute for God's

---

[16]. "List of Mental Disorders," *Wikipedia*, January 8, 2018, https://en.wikipedia.org/w/index.php?title=List_of_mental_disorders&oldid=819292528.

grace at least in our own minds. It follows then that if my efforts are so great and they reflect the great depth of my devotion to Him, yours must also indicate your spiritual condition as well. It's easy to see how subjective our judgments of each other can become.

The virtues that we value highest are those that we ourselves work the hardest to cultivate, but they may not be the same as yours. My own judgment of your heart is unfair and unjust because I may place a different value upon its works than you. As I have said before, it is the Lord's opinion that matters, not yours or mine. Our psychological stability and therefore our judgment is certainly under question.

The Woman Caught in Adultery

Probably the closest insight to the Lord's view on Christian attitude towards judgment comes from the story of the woman caught in adultery. This sin is obvious and easy for us to identify in a person's life because there are usually witnesses either to the act or to the circumstances surrounding it. Sometimes it's not just simply the confession of the person accused, but there is the partner as well. Such liaisons generally do not stay hidden forever. Sooner or later the facts present themselves. This is why it's so easy to declare someone guilty. The woman was caught by the Pharisees in the very act and had no excuse or defense.

The Pharisees took the situation before Jesus in an attempt to place Him in a dilemma before the people. The law of Moses required the execution of the woman by stoning, but it was well known that Jesus taught forgiveness and restoration. The Pharisees hoped to catch Him between His words and the law of Moses, but Jesus understood the situation. There was no conflict in His mind at all, only a certain disappointment in the lack of wisdom of the Pharisees.

The answer is simple. If the defendant has no value or significance to us, execution of sentence can become a self-righteous thing rather than an emotional dilemma, at least in our own minds. It feels good to have control over someone else. We feel powerful and important. This becomes pride, the thing God hates the most. All we have to do is quell our own guilty consciences. Jesus knows this all too well, and He uses it to convict the Pharisees of their pride and self-righteousness. The following is the account.

> But Jesus went to the Mount of Olives. Now early in the morning He came again into the temple, and all the people came to Him; and He sat down and taught them. Then the scribes and Pharisees brought to Him a woman caught in adultery. And when they had set her in the midst, they said to Him, "Teacher, this woman was caught in adultery, in the very act. Now

Moses, in the law, commanded us that such should be stoned. But what do You say?" This they said, testing Him, that they might have something of which to accuse Him. But Jesus stooped down and wrote on the ground with His finger, as though He did not hear. So when they continued asking Him, He raised Himself up and said to them, "He who is without sin among you, let him throw a stone at her first." And again He stooped down and wrote on the ground. Then those who heard it, being convicted by their conscience, went out one by one, beginning with the oldest even to the last. And Jesus was left alone, and the woman standing in the midst. When Jesus had raised Himself up and saw no one but the woman, He said to her, "Woman, where are those accusers of yours? Has no one condemned you?" She said, "No one, Lord." And Jesus said to her, "Neither do I condemn you; go and sin no more." (John 8:1–12, NKJV)

The woman was guilty. This point is undeniable. The very irrefutability focuses our minds on the question of punishment. This is not a question regarding opinions of her character but on the fact of her guilt. The law does not leave the decision open for discussion. It required her execution, end of story.

But the execution of that judgment fell upon those who had the authority to do so. This would have been the responsibility of a legal ecclesiastic court, not a self-righteous, vigilante mob manipulated by hypocrites. But Jesus made His point even to a lynch mob. The individual mob participants (even though they were all in agreement) had no right to judge the woman and carry out sentence. Those who were unrighteous should not sentence others who like themselves are also unrighteous. It is a question of the authority of people to judge, condemn, and execute the law of God in other people's lives. Jesus makes it clear with His comments, "He who is without sin among you, let him throw a stone at her first." The conflict was between the self-righteous mob authority of the Pharisees versus the legal ecclesiastic court and the woman's right to a just trial.

The key to understanding what happened is found in verse 7. It is not the accuracy of the charge (this seems to be beyond question). It is not the righteousness of the law of God. It is not the severity of the sentence. It is not even the dilemma of grace versus law. It is the authority of the accusers. The question is the right of the mob to accuse, judge, and execute sentence. Did the duly recognized legal authority have the right through due process of law to pass judgment on the woman? Absolutely, but the people who stood in judgment over this woman were not the legal authority. They were people just like her who as Jesus pointed out were guilty of their own transgressions. Their authority was merely self-righteous indignation, and that is not enough. Jesus used this reality to show their own guilt and to reveal the need for restraint among the crowd. The result was the freedom of the woman and perhaps a realization among her accusers that individual, personal judgment of the sin of others is unrighteous and unjust. Love doesn't even seem to come into play, but it does because Jesus teaches the Pharisees a powerful lesson in humility. Showing a good man his error is regarded as a loving act.

Pharisaism: A Substitute for True Righteousness

It seems that people that are most concerned with living holy and righteously exclude everything else. We write covenants and demand signatures of acceptance to ensure that those who come into the church are not just born again but in full cooperation with our ideas of righteous Christian behavior. I know the reason why. It is to ensure that there is no possibility of criticism of our own Pharisaism and to ensure that newcomers are equally duplicitous. Like the Pharisees, we try to make our acolytes like us. We truly love to argue most with those who are truly in full agreement with us. It makes us feel superior when no one disagrees.

It is much easier to establish a set of rules or a code of conduct that is purely subjective than it is to do the thing that is commanded by the Lord. That thing is to love with the love that Christ had for us when He went to the cross. That is tough and cannot be signed and sworn to. It must be practiced in everyday thinking and living.

Such love doesn't come from just deciding to "love." It is not built upon dogged determination as obedience is, even though persistence is necessary. It is a matter of perseverance but of a gentler sort. It must not spring from a desire to do the right thing but to be the right person. It is not a set of instructions to follow but a way of life characterized by constant surrender and submission. Not just to the rules but also to the truth about the very nature of every (including our own) human soul which lusts to envy, covet, and self-serve. Why do we persist in belittling others? Is it so that we can feel superior about ourselves? Or is it merely to preemptively defend ourselves?

This may seem a strange thing to a reader, but yes, it is surrender to our understanding of the nature of our own souls—not in licentiousness but to the awareness of who we are. It is a giving up of the battle so to speak and casting away the false hope that we can succeed in defeating that baser part of ourselves in our own effort. I speak not of myself alone either but about everyone. "All have sinned and come short of the glory of God" (Romans 3:23, NKJV). We are all of a wicked, selfish nature, and the indulgence of our own lust is the path of destruction. No, the answer is surrender and submission to the fact that we are sinners and not to the desires that tempt us.

The first step to conquering any self-inflicted disability is to recognize it, confess it to God, and admit our responsibility. It is a long road to recovery from there, but it is necessary to make the first step on any extended journey.

The Revelation of the Human Spirit

The mature Christian accepts practical holiness as prerequisite, yet he does not dwell upon it. He focuses upon the need of others to recognize Jesus Christ as the only hope for deliverance even as Paul said, "I thank God—through Jesus Christ our Lord! So then, with the mind I myself serve the law of God, but with the flesh the law of sin" (Romans 7:25, NKJV).

We must know the nature of the natural man. We must recognize the holiness that is God. We must submit to His help. We must study and internalize Spirit-filled and Spirit-controlled Christianity in light of the Word, being filled with the love of Christ. This is what Christian maturity is all about.

Some would suggest that if I live according the law, I will fulfill the task that the Lord has set for me on earth. But unfortunately, such an understanding of the law is merely a perversion of the facts of what Jesus taught.

The problem is that in order to achieve the desired result, I must believe that I am making progress that I have conquered the flesh and its desire to disregard the law. Therein is the great danger, the self-delusion. We can never reach that desired result. The flesh is an integrated part of who we are. We will never shed this part of our nature while in this "body of death" as Paul labels it.

At this point most people say, "Why not? I don't lie, I don't steal, I don't covet, and I'm a lot better than so and so." It is the same mistake the Pharisees made who tried and judged the adulterous woman. Such devotion is misguided and is reflected by our perceived holiness and does not make us perfect nor should it convince anyone else of our perfection.

If I make judgments about my practices of righteousness or those of others from a standard that I have not created (God's Law), then it is impossible for me to judge righteously. The law has already judged that I myself am guilty. It doesn't matter which commandment because if I am guilty of part, I am guilty of all.

Only Righteousness Can Judge Righteousness

It might be argued that a judge of the court does not create civil law, yet he judges it. But I would say that he is a creator of the law, maybe not personally, but as a representative of the legislators whose natures are shared by him.

The civil laws of the land are created by fallible, imperfect human beings and therefore must be judged through reason and circumstance. God's law comes from His perfect and divine nature and cannot be reasonably approached with human standards of reason. But can we not judge actions according to God's law? Yes, and we must. I am the only human being who knows my own heart and has the right to honestly judge my true motivations. In other words, God and I are the only ones who can see the condition of my heart. There is exception in the matter of legal, authorized, ecclesiastical verdicts by fallible people. Such judgments are righteous and in accordance with Scripture. For example, I refer to Peter's judgment as the leader of the church in Jerusalem of Annanias and Sephira.

Is the Law the True Righteous Standard?

At this point, we must decide if the law really is perfect or not. If it is to be the standard of righteousness, then it must be perfectly righteous. If not, then all actions judged by it can be argued. Hence, a need arises for a court to decide on the validity of the arguments, and one opinion is as valid as another.

I would say that the law of God is the expressed perfection of God and, therefore, is binding on all of His creation. In other words, He is the Creator, and His rules must be obeyed by his creation. The alternative is to deny

His sovereignty and His pure nature. Therefore, He alone can truly judge since even my own judgments of myself are flawed. Sometimes I am not aware even of my own subjectivity. Perfection cannot be judged by imperfection, only accepted. If I am ever guilty of any infraction at any time, then I am by definition a transgressor of the law and therefore, imperfect and incapable of impartial judgment. My failures disqualify me from the position of judge because I cannot make an independent ruling on my own compliance, let alone someone else's. I inevitably grant to myself grace when grace cannot be authoritatively given.

If I cannot judge, why does God say, "Be ye Holy for I am Holy"? We must first clarify holiness. Holiness is a state of separation. It is a quality of our Divine Father and declares Him completely separated from evil. Therefore, it includes a moral element in which the state of holiness means removed from sin and worldly contamination. The key to understanding "holiness" does not lie in day-by-day, minute-by-minute evaluations of the purity of an action or thought but more in a state of mind or way of life based upon the realization that I am totally without merit by virtue of my inadequate self-righteousness before the law and the full holiness of God. The sacrifices made in the temple to God were holy because they were separated to God. Yet the meat and the valuables were taken by the priests and used for their own compensation and the maintenance of the temple. This was commanded by God and known by all the worshippers.

But the moral law or the law of Moses (the Ten Commandments and all the other laws) is perfect without exception and forces me to the statement, "I am a transgressor, and I ask for forgiveness and mercy." It is by God's grace that the request is granted never by works, efforts, or even an earned credit balance of good deeds. A focused constant pursuit of holiness forces me to be self-aware and in a constant conscious state of repentance. How can I minister to and empathize with others when all I have on my mind is my own failures? Welcome to the world of "living by the law."

I cannot be effective to a world that is overcome with selfishness by focusing upon myself. I cannot remove the mote in my brother's eye while blinded by the beam in my own. I must be "other-centered" to minister effectively, not introverted by my failures.

If purity is the primary goal of my Christian walk, how can I ever succeed? If my life is spent in a constant pursuit of purity and I know that the level of purity of my life will never be acceptable nor on par with the holiness that has been imputed to me by faith in Jesus Christ, am I not headed for defeat? Why would God show me Christian maturity in stages of progress knowing that I can never attain sufficient purity to proceed to the next level?

I would forever be stuck in the first grade. There must be another focus for my effort.

Holiness, sanctification, consecration, and purity are all related. But, in a human sense, all must be separated. Holiness is purely an attribute of God which we are to emulate. I am only holy because I have been given a position of holiness by the Lord God extending to me His own holiness through the sanctifying work of the indwelling Holy Spirit. Sanctification is the act of separating ourselves to God and away from the world, accomplished by the Holy Spirit. Consecration is a formal act in which separation is established strictly for God's use. Purity means separation from sin and therefore, by default, from all that is not godly. Holiness then is the condition, not the act. It is a noun not a verb. Sanctification is two parts. The first is done by the Holy Spirit, is without our interference, and is called positional sanctification by the theologians. The second part is where we make life choices to separate ourselves from the world.

Jesus teaches a parable on this very subject. He doesn't even comment on it. Being the Lord of all, He knew the minds of men. His words penetrated their souls and they understood exactly what He was saying.

> Also He spoke this parable to some who trusted in themselves that they were righteous, and despised others: "Two

men went up to the temple to pray, one a Pharisee and the other a tax collector. The Pharisee stood and prayed thus with himself, 'God, I thank You that I am not like other men—extortioners, unjust, adulterers, or even as this tax collector. I fast twice a week; I give tithes of all that I possess.' And the tax collector, standing afar off, would not so much as raise his eyes to heaven, but beat his breast, saying, 'God, be merciful to me a sinner!' I tell you, this man went down to his house justified rather than the other; for everyone who exalts himself will be humbled, and he who humbles himself will be exalted." (Luke 18:9–14, NKJV)

The conclusion is unmistakable. It is the recognition of responsibility for personal sin and repentance that brings the attention of the Lord, not acts of righteousness. This is called contrition. Can the Pharisee correctly think himself to be holy to God because of his acts? Jesus Himself said no. But is Pharisaism commendable? Without doubt, the answer is yes. Jesus said, "Therefore whatever they tell you to observe, that observe and do, but do not do according to their works; for they say, and do not do" (Matthew 23:3, NKJV).

Am I to disregard acts of righteousness or works? Absolutely not, James tells us that our works of righteousness are the result of our faith. Our works are to be done, not for proving righteousness but as acts of devotion.

The solution for the problem has baffled God's people for centuries. Some say that the Christian life is a constant pursuit of purity. Others say that human depravity discounts the possibility of purity and therefore relieves us to live licentiously. Neither extreme can be true. There must be someplace in the middle where we should be. Paul describes and condemns this very thinking in chapter 6 of Romans.

Maybe we can find the answer in a comparison of Christian virtues which can give us insight. Faith, for instance, might be a good place to begin. We know that the faith of a baby Christian is not as deep as the faith of one who has walked with the Lord for many years (in most cases). The reason is that mature Christians have spent time in reconciling their understanding of faith with their experiences as people who have lived in a sinful world. We know that we have been promised eternal life, but it is a fact that all die. Jesus said, "So the Lord said, 'If you have faith as a mustard seed, you can say to this mulberry tree, 'Be pulled up by the roots and be planted in the sea, and it would obey you'" (Luke 17:6, NKJV), but none of us have rearranged the geography of our planet. Are we then saved or not? Further, Scripture tells us that our Heavenly

Father knows that we have need of food and shelter, yet He tells us, "Seek first the kingdom of heaven and His righteousness, and all these things will be added unto you" (Matthew 6:33, NKJV), but we all have to work or we and our families starve. Even so, we are still saved.

In "holiness," we have similar situations. The law says, "Thou shalt love the Lord thy God with all thy strength, with all thy heart, and with all thy mind" (Matthew 12:29–31, NKJV). Who among us can fully comply with such a commandment? Perhaps sometimes loving the Lord is foremost in our minds but all the time? I think not. We then are guilty if we do not all the time. We are told, "Obey every ordinance of man." But who can be aware of every law that is written? Do we not excuse ourselves by saying, "Who can remember all those laws?" Yes, but God is clear, sin is not acceptable.

Can we live in full compliance to the law of God? No. So then how much compliance is holy, and how much is not? Some say, "Well, these are sins of omission, not commission, so the line must be drawn at willful sin." A question arises then. What if there is a choice between legal compliance and love? A sign is placed at a favorite swimming hole saying, "No swimming by order of the Health Department." We arrive and find one of our friends out in the deep portion drowning. If we jump in to save him, we are breaking the law of man and therefore the law of God. Is this sin? Yes. Do I dive in any way? Yes, but I am guilty of willful sin nonetheless. In Exodus, the first chapter, the Hebrew midwives were ordered to kill all the male babies at birth. They lied telling the Egyptian authorities that the women gave birth before their arrival. The Scripture says their houses were blessed for all generations.

These examples reveal the futility of living by the law. Living by grace is not a moment-by-moment evaluation of the application of the law to our "holiness" but a state of willingness to conform ourselves to the will of God. The indwelling Holy Spirit is a product of the grace of God in our lives through the gift of love that came to us by faith in Jesus Christ. He convicts and teaches us. This becomes a life-long project on His part. The new place of the law in the lives of believers is in Hebrews 10:15–17.

> And the Holy Spirit also testifies to us; for after saying, "This is the covenant that I will make with them after those days, says the Lord: I will put my laws upon their heart, and on their mind, I will write them," He then says, "And their sins and their lawless deeds I will remember no more." (NKJV)

Rather than being a conscious observance we now find because of the grace of God in the indwelling manifestation of the Holy Spirit, the moral law is incorporated into our very being. But to make ourselves follow the law consciously for righteousness' sake is a breach of our covenant with grace. Essentially, we have created the eleventh commandment, "Thou shalt do your best to keep the law, and God will surely forgive you for your efforts." This is not grace, it is self-made law. The method of grace is to show us the choices, and then tell us which is righteous. The internalized law reveals itself to us when we are presented with a choice between right and wrong. It is grace that assures us of joy when we choose to listen to that internal urging not the law.

I would hope that we would be convinced that living by the law is impossible. So what is it that God expects from us? He expects us to go beyond worrying about the details of legalism. He has a process for us to reach maturity of which "holiness" is only the first step. As Paul says in Romans 12:1, "I beseech you therefore, brethren, by the mercies of God, that you present your bodies a living sacrifice, holy, acceptable to God, which is your reasonable service" (NKJV).

Holiness is then a "reasonable" service, but what is meant by "reasonable"? "Reasonable service" is sometimes translated "spiritual service" or "spiritual act of service." Either way, the idea is of a foundational or fundamental aspect of our Christianity. The very basic element of Christianity, at least in the eyes of the world, is to be an "ambassador" for Christ, to purport ourselves as examples of human virtue. Why would a nonbeliever place any credibility in Christianity if we act in lust the same way he does? When we associate ourselves with the Christian worldview, we immediately invite inspection. The world wants to know if Christianity is truly valid for us or are we just hypocrites?

As "living sacrifices" we willfully submit our passions and desires for the sake of the testimony of Christ. If I respect my parents and my family, I will not do anything to cast aspersions on them. I will do the right thing to protect their reputations. It is the most fundamental aspect of integrity. Chuck Swindoll lists examples of integrity violations that show an epidemic of little publicized infractions including impaired-driving deaths, AIDS, sexual scandals in the military and politics, and sadly, religious leaders.[17] Holiness then becomes the basic quality of my Christian testimony. I separate myself from the world as an act of devotion and reverence for my Savior. As Paul says in Romans 12:2, "And do not be conformed to this world, but be transformed by the renewing of your mind, that you may prove what is that good and acceptable and perfect will of God" (NKJV). But this is a far cry from, depending on the law for my salvation, sanctification and God's Love.

For these things, I must depend on grace. The full manifestation of God in the Christian life is evidenced by

---

[17.] Charles R. Swindoll, *Rise & Shine: A Wake-up Call* (Portland, Or: Multnomah, 1989), 188–189.

divine love provided by God Himself and brought out by personal diligence as described in 2 Peter 1: 3ff.

When I was in school, I was taught the theme of the book of Romans by some of my teachers as, "The just shall live by his faith" (Habakkuk 2:4, NKJV). I know the statement is true but what of the meaning? Living by faith must cover so much more than intellectual assent. It means having the same focus as Christ, not failure of complying with the law but in seeing other's needs and seeking ways to help fulfill those needs.

Others say that the theme of the entire Bible is Jesus. It is considered by these men to be the hermeneutic for the entire Word of God to man. They concluded that everything was written to reveal Him to us, and I believe this to be true as well after a fashion. But if the broader theme is Jesus then the meaning or the theme of Romans cannot be limited just to faith alone. It must incorporate the greater theme as well. Faith defined as the result of the will alone cannot provide sufficient coverage to explain the entire scope of God's Word. As I read and studied God's Word more, I began to realize the detail that makes the idea that Jesus as the primary theme of the Bible possible. It is that Jesus is the embodiment of God's divine sacrificial love.

The Essence of Spiritual Leadership

So what is the true standard of spiritual maturity? This question has been the source of countless books and articles regarding discipleship and spiritual formation. When I inspected the library of a well-known Christian university, I found no less than forty-three books listed on spiritual formation. Certainly, there are many more not in that particular collection. Have we missed the mark? Why have so many titles covered the subject, yet we seem unable to solve the problem?

I believe there are very few pastors who would not tell us that the essence of true spirituality is love. They see Christianity as a practical, day-by-day experience. Certainly, this separates them from the academics who are more concerned with the technical aspects of religion. Pastors are on the front lines and know what is important for believers to mature and to "walk worthy of the Gospel" in sight of the world. No other characteristic that is visible to human beings is more telling and a more certain proof of the presence of the Holy Spirit's control of our lives than love. Certainly, righteous living is also an indication, but love will incorporate holiness from a compulsion to obedience that true devotion espouses. It was apparent from the Lord's words that righteous living can be faked. The Pharisees were good at it, but their hearts were not right.

Therefore, looking only for separated living can fool us, but love is undeniably from God.

"The one who loves is of God for God is love." It is the truest reflection of Him in us. When we see great Christian endeavor, we should take a second look. If love is present in the actions then we may safely say that God is at work in that person's life. Without it, we are just "a sounding brass or a tinkling cymbal."

True spirituality begins with the examples of loving leaders. For centuries, the church, and by this, I mean its leadership, has judged the spiritual condition of individuals by many different methods. The early church at Corinth based its opinions on the observable manifestations of the miraculous spiritual gifts (1 Corinthians 12–14). Others in the same church were judging based upon the candidate's associations with well-known contemporary church leaders (1 Corinthians 1:12–13). Many of the churches judged based upon letters of recommendation from the apostles. But in each of these situations, the judgments boiled down to personal observations of mature Christians whether in that local church or by those recommending to it. In modern times, we must make judgments as well. The problem is that with mass communication at the level of efficiency that it is today, normal processes of discrimination are either bypassed or short-circuited. It is very easy for TV producers and directors to assume the role of a church leader and judge based purely upon charisma or photogenic value. So many elements enter into the decisions of these persons that it must be a most difficult process for the righteous to balance them with the mission of the ministry. They are responsible for millions of dollars in salary, equipment, legal advisors, logistics etc., provided by many different sponsors, corporate, as well as individual. For this reason, producers fear alienating these segments of their audience since they must grab the audience's attention and hold it. It must be a temptation to avoid some of the more difficult spiritual aspects of ministry to accommodate these massive pressures. These difficulties may include the discretionary processes which ensure the subject's spiritual maturity and suitability to lead Christian ministries (see 1 Timothy 3:1ff). Perhaps it is easier to place a charismatic baby Christian out front rather than an older, more seasoned saint of somewhat less notoriety.

We have seen those who have done great things in God's name and judged them to be great Christian men and women. Some have been average people, and some have been people of authority, position, and fame. But in our desire to see the hand of God working in a lost world, we rush too quickly to elevate some. We see newly converted Christians who because of their success in secular endeavors draw tremendous recognition from the world. This quality may make them suitable for broadcast success, but prominence in the secular world does not mean that they are great leaders in the Christian world.

These situations hurt the church and hurt the individual. We place tremendous pressure on these people to live lives of absolute Christianity and quickly accuse when their spiritual maturity is not sufficient to resist the kind of temptation that comes with fame. It is easy for such people to fall into the same methods of operation that made them secular successes yet not presenting Christian ideals as prominently as they should. Christian maturity involves both discernment and discrimination tempered by love.

The qualities of a good leader are built through years of experiencing the love of God. Love tempers our baser leanings. It calls us to closeness with our God and familiarity with His ways. It reminds us that "His ways are not our ways" to deny ourselves and to practice His Word. It gives us the discernment to make difficult even painful decisions that will benefit the kingdom of God and not ourselves even though another choice may be more comfortable for everyone concerned.

We must be more discriminating about who we endorse, or we will suffer a severe crippling of the church's ability to self-govern and destruction of our credibility as the people of God. It takes spiritual maturity to deal with the temptations that so easily shipwreck us. Lust begins in the heart and works its way out into our actions, but who among us has not experienced that devastating truth? We are human beings with that most self-destructive of all weapons, the sinful nature. We all have found ourselves in just such a place. But the sad fact is that the higher we are carried, the farther we have to fall, meaning that the more prominent our fall becomes in the eyes of others.

Loving Leadership Involves Righteous Judgment

We wish to see God working in the earth to such an extent that we are willing to proclaim from the highest mountaintop that ours is the great and magnificent God and to declare the most uncertain of human actions to be righteous. A recent TV series pictured a pastor and his family in everyday life situations. The counsel and actions that he gave were a conglomeration of every religion and "feel-good" psychology popular today. Christians were quick to hail the program as a great leap for the cause of Christ in Hollywood. We were so happy that finally the things we hold dear were being portrayed by Hollywood in a favorable light. But we completely overlooked the fact that the Bible is rarely ever referred to, and the name of Jesus was not said at all. What kind of a victory is that?

Why then do we find ourselves so disappointed and even disillusioned by the failures of those whom we trusted and respected? We watch, and we do not criticize. We do not correct or admonish, and the result is disappointment. The most basic act of love that a parent shows is loving discipline which involves correction.

We can only judge those actions which are revealed to us in life. We cannot make assumptions. This is the judgment that Jesus warns us about. Our judgments must be made based on certainty and not feelings or opinions of others. "If it swims and quacks, it must be a duck" is a very fallible means of judgment and surely offensive to coots and teals. But the world has a way of making us feel guilty, critical, and intolerant when we try to correct ourselves biblically. The cry is heard loud and clear, "Judge not lest ye be judged." This and "God helps those who help themselves" are probably the most frequent attempts by the world to squelch reproof, rebuke, and admonition of the behavior among our younger (spiritually not physically) Christians.

• CHAPTER •
5

THE PROCESS OF SPIRITUAL GROWTH

What is God's purpose in discipleship but to make us Christlike? Why does He want to do this? What does it mean to be Christlike? I recently attended a Sunday school class at the invitation of a friend. As I listened, the Sunday school teacher read from the denominational lesson plan and began to speak about spiritual development. He said that God wants us to be Christian but not to give up our individuality. He proudly declared that we should be Christian but still the same person. I found myself asking him what he thought being Christlike meant. I continued on and said that God wanted us to be conformed to the image of Christ. What room is left for individuality? "For I am crucified with Christ it is no longer I but Christ who lives in me…" (Galatians 2:20, NKJV). It was not his answer that concerned me for he seemed uncertain and unable to reply. It was the sudden and passionate response of others, who angrily took issue with me, that shocked me the most. It was apparent to me that I had unwittingly hit upon a nerve.

One woman in particular, who was a youth worker, took exception to my words and suggested that I had no idea what I was talking about. She said Jesus wants us to come to Him just as we are and that the idea of submersing oneself into Christianity to the point of losing my identity was misguided. I told her that my Bible clearly wants me to come to Christ for salvation, but there is a huge amount of instruction on how I am to put the old man to death that Christ might live His life through me. How else would the world know that there is life in Christ at all?

The old man that I was and still can be is the farthest thing from Christ imaginable. He is self-indulgent, argumentative, angry, and spiteful. He is a very unhappy individual. Yet in contrast, Jesus loves. His love for us is overwhelming and beyond description. I desire to be that way. I want no part of the sadness that is the carnal me. I want peace and hope and charity to be the watchwords of my testimony. God puts within us a desire to be Christlike. He wants others to see Christ within us. He wants Christ to be the first thing they see. The reason He does this is simple. He loves them just as He loved us (John 3:16). The shift from law to grace came by Jesus.

> Nevertheless, knowing that a man is not justified by the works of the Law but

> through faith in Christ Jesus, even we have believed in Christ Jesus, so that we may be justified by faith in Christ and not by the works of the Law; since by the works of the Law no flesh will be justified. (Galatians 2:16, NKJV)

Spiritual growth comes from two primary areas. The first is God's plan, and second is our own willingness to obey and conform ourselves to it. The Scripture gives a step-by-step process for our growth and the desired end result. Our growth begins first of all with God's part in securing for us the power to accomplish growth. This power comes directly from Him by promises that He has made to us. The fulfillment of these promises comes directly from the fact of God's integrity. The Scripture records this certainty, "In hope of eternal life which God, who cannot lie, promised before time began" (Titus 1:2, NKJV).

It is in 2 Peter that we see the importance of these promises to the growth process. In verse 1, Peter tells us that he shares our faith. He is careful to mention that this faith comes because of the sinless obedience of Jesus Christ who went to the cross and accomplished the work of atonement for us. In the next verse, he tells us that knowledge of Jesus Christ is the means to grace and peace. For our part, this is the greatest benefit of being a child of God. It is a statement of assurance and indication of the thing that our soul cries out for the most. Swindoll says, "There is nothing—absolutely nothing—of greater importance than knowing Christ intensely and intimately."[18] Peace means a life of satisfaction and completeness. Grace means the goodwill and help of the Father in heaven. Peter further states that the continued increase of the knowledge of Jesus Christ assures of continued peace.

He follows with the assurance that these promises will grant to us all that we need to fulfill our complete spiritual growth by making us full partakers of His divine nature. Since the divine nature is love, it seems reasonable to deduce that divine love is the end result of the process.

If all has been provided to us through grace for life and peace and all that we need has already been given to us, then why are we "burning out"? Wonderful, loving, mature, godly people are dropping like flies all around us. Jesus told us, "Come unto me all ye that labor and are heavy laden and I will give you rest. Take my yoke upon you and learn of me for I am meek and lowly of heart and you shall receive rest unto your soul. For my yoke is easy and my burden is light" (Matthew 11:28ff, NKJV). EASY? LIGHT? Is He serious? Of course, He is. Why then are we burning out? Chuck Swindoll records the cry of a sad minister, "'Nobody around me knows this, but I'm operat-

---

[18] Charles R Swindoll, *Intimacy with the Almighty: Encountering Christ in the Secret Places of Your Life* (Nashville, Tenn.: J. Countryman, 1999), 22.

ing on fumes. I am lonely, hollow, shallow, and enslaved to a schedule that never lets up.' As I embraced him and affirmed his vulnerability and honesty, he began to weep with deep, heaving sobs"[19] Once again, the answer is simple. We are not carrying the yoke properly. We are straining under the burden that is unbearable because we are denying the means by which it can be made easy.

Our problem is that, just like our battle with the flesh, we focus upon this detail and that. We take our eyes off of our Lord, shield and buckler, and we jump into the fray without patience or restraint. We forget that all things should be done with moderation. We're like the truck in the mud; the driver with his foot to the floorboard slinging mud thirty feet into the air and going nowhere. Soon bearings, gears, and other parts give out, and the result is a useless chunk of metal with tires stuck in the same spot. Jesus has provided us with all we need for life and godliness. We must allow Him to provide us with the tools and the methods. We should focus on our relationship with Him and allow Him to put us in the place we need to be and to help us to recognize it. I don't need to attack the problem. All I need to do is stay on the path of spiritual growth, and the things that are for me to do will align themselves with me. In no other way will the yoke be easy and the burden light.

One of the failings I have noticed of young men is the frantic and aggressive way in which they do their work. It's

---

[19.] Swindoll. Intimacy with the Almighty (1999), 8

like all of this pent-up energy bursts forth when faced with a challenge. It must be a quality of youth. They are like the furious efforts of the truck stuck in the mud. But as they grow older, their forehead gets sore from beating it against a concrete wall. Soon they slow down and look before they leap. They let the lessons of maturity and patience guide their steps. They find that solutions and efforts become more successful and less frantic and worrisome.

As Christians, the same thing happens. The difference is that the Savior does the work for us. Why worry and be anxious? He has told us that if we will focus on Him that He will guide our steps and direct us in our paths. We just have to submit to being guided. "My yoke is easy, and my burden is light."

Spiritual maturity is a process. It begins with the first step and continues on reviewing previous steps and honing growth skills. It is a process that is built upon the previous step, and the next step is built upon it. Each step is a progression to the next. In Christianity, the ultimate goal is to be Christlike, of course, it is necessary to know who Christ is, and what it is to be Christlike. To be Christlike requires first that we know Him. Two Peter tells us that this knowledge must be obtained.

> Simon Peter, a bondservant and apostle of Jesus Christ, To those who have obtained like precious faith with us by the righ-

teousness of our God and Savior Jesus Christ: Grace and peace be multiplied to you in the knowledge of God and of Jesus our Lord. (2 Peter 1:1, NKJV)

Knowing Christ is much more than just familiarity with the details of His life and ministry on earth. It is knowing Him in an experiential way. It is the way that a close disciple knows His master/teacher. It is the knowledge of the personal. As one would know a friend that we speak to on a regular basis, we must know Him. When I call up a friend or family member, I know them. I recognize their voice. I understand what they mean by "How ya doin?" It is a familiarity that comes from personal, intimate association.

The Bible teaches us that God chooses to introduce us through the Gospel, the illumination of the Holy Spirit and the testimony of others who have already met Him. We are introduced and then when, by faith, we accept Him as Lord and Savior, we find ourselves empowered by God to grow in the knowledge of Jesus. This is how this knowledge is obtained. Through our personal knowledge of Jesus, God shows us by the accounts we read in the Bible about His life. He grants to us more personal and intimate knowledge as we are invited into His thoughts and feelings as expressed in these accounts. The Holy Spirit takes these accounts and gives us emotive reactions so that we begin to understand Jesus's feelings and concerns. We get to know

Him. The Holy Spirit continues to guide us in increasing our knowledge by encouraging others to expound on the teachings that Christ began. Writers such as Paul and Peter and the other apostles help us to further gain insight by expressing their own experiences as Christ, the Holy Spirit has helped them. We, ourselves, experience Christ as the Holy Spirit leads, protects, convicts, and encourages us personally. This is what is meant by a personal, intimate knowledge of Jesus Christ.

Perhaps the difficulty arises because we cannot see Him and hear His physical voice and identify inflections of emotion in His tone that we recognize in a conversation with anyone with whom we have spoken frequently. That is, however, one reason why faith is so important in Christianity. Our God is personal, and He wants to have personal dealings with us. But we must accept the limitations of such a relationship and make the proper allowances that God has provided us. He has promised us that, "I will never leave you nor forsake you" (Hebrews 13:5). He has sent to us the Holy Spirit to be our Helper helping our understanding and our faith.

The help God gives is not only assurance and hope in our future but individual guidance as to how to live in a way that is not only pleasing to Him but beneficial to us. This guidance is also what makes personal ministry and service effective. He provides us with great promises for this help and assures us that He cannot lie.

• CHAPTER •
6

Factors Which Contribute to Spiritual Growth

The first is God's grace. Grace means a lot of things to a lot of people, but what we wish to focus on here is what God means by grace. Of course, the old adage, "The unmerited favor of God" is accurate, but it takes a lot of thinking to apply it specifically to Christian growth. Grace, in this context, means "help" even when we don't know we need it and certainly don't deserve it. It's like the "Help" button on your computer. It means constant availability and information. God has promised us this, and He wants us to avail ourselves of it. The greatest help, of course, is the Holy Spirit. Jesus even calls Him the "Helper" (παράκλητος). He promised His coming to help us (John 15:26).

In Peter's introduction to his second epistle, he makes clear the first step in our growth process and tells us that help comes from God Himself.

> As His divine power has given to us all things that pertain to life and godliness, through the knowledge of Him who called us by glory and virtue, by which have been given to us exceedingly great and precious promises, that through these you may be partakers of the divine nature, having escaped the corruption that is in the world through lust. (2 Peter 1:3–4, NKJV.)

By the knowledge of Jesus Christ, we receive all the tools we need to become Christlike. The little phrase, "pertaining to life and godliness," plugs us in not only to survival tools but also to growth and ministry tools. It is not His intention to save us, call us friends, and then abandon us. He knows that we have nothing by which we can cope in a lost world in a Christian way, so He "helps" us out. And not just a few simple helps but "everything" we need. The means by which He does this is amazing. It is not just the latest "self-help" book or the newest TV preacher or even the latest and greatest ministry but by making us partakers in the divine nature itself. Now that is truly amazing. Not just outward tools but a change in our entire nature which allows us to see things from His perspective. His knowledge is not merely head knowledge but the attributes of God Himself which will help us to make righteous decisions and say helpful and comforting things as needed. It helps us to recognize sin and wickedness not only in ourselves but in the world around us thereby avoiding it like a plague.

The ancient Chinese proverb tells us that the journey of a thousand miles begins with the first step. There is also a first step on the road to spiritual maturity. It is the step that changes everything. It is the means by which all the promises of God to the Christian are made available. It is faith.

Not just a reasonable understanding of who Christ was as a historical figure but the certainty of Christ as a living person who can be known and communicated with in a personal way as friend to friend right now.

CHAPTER 7

Faith

> Trust in the Lord with all your heart,
> And do not lean on your own understanding.
> In all your ways acknowledge Him,
> And He will make your paths straight.
> —Proverbs 3:5, NKJV

C. S. Lewis asks in his book *Mere Christianity*, "In what sense is faith a virtue?", and on the next page, he answers his own question, "Now Faith, in the sense in which I am here using the word, is the art of holding on to things your reason has once accepted, in spite of your changing moods."[20] Our faith should not change from day to day or from circumstance to circumstance. Situations change, our faith should not.

We awaken in the morning to the sound of electronic beeping as our alarm clock reminds us of our obligations.

[20.] Lewis, *Mere Christianity*. 123.

Through bleary eyes, we barely focus and then manage to gaze at the display and realize we can snooze a minute or two more. We continue the process of awakening when rudely the clock repeats its annoying reminder. We tumble out and stumble to the kitchen where a preprogrammed coffee maker has begun its simple and necessary task of following its digital command to make coffee of the right temperature and strength to satisfy our need to awaken and begin the duties of the day. Moving on, we jump into the shower where a water heater has already prepared the water to the temperature necessary for cleanliness and other mundane tasks necessary to keep a modern household working. A pump somewhere in another part of the city has started and pressurized a pipe with clean purified water delivering it to our house in such a way as to flow the amount of water necessary for our ablutions. We climb into our autos, starting the engine and moving out into traffic. As we turn the steering wheel and administer the accelerator, we pick up speed and blend in with the hundreds of others who have done the same thing. The machine responds as expected, and we drive on. We control our vehicles this way in an attempt to remain within the law and the rules of the road. Our expectation is that we will arrive safely at our destination without incident or interruption.

 The amazing machines of our modern world have become so effective and dependable that we hardly give them a second thought. Yet one hundred years ago, our lives would have seemed awe-inspiring if not downright supernatural to anyone who lived then. We do not think about the faulty alarm clock or the power failure or any number of unpredictable and unforeseeable catastrophes that could ruin our day if not our very lives. We have faith in our machines.

Faith as Part of Daily Life

I fear I have opened a can of worms here as we shift our thinking to a realm fraught with uncertainty. It is a reminder of how fragile our lives really are.

We arrive at our place of work and greet the boss, who unexpectedly berates us for having been delinquent in our duty the previous day. We are shocked as our expectations for the day have been shattered, and the routine is now disrupted. We left the house that morning with a belief that everything was as it should be, yet on the road, the car stalls and grinds to a halt with a sickening whine of metal tearing itself apart. In both of these situations, our expectations were shattered because our faith in the status quo had been broken.

We pull out our cell phones and call a tow which drags us to our mechanic who says those words we dread to here, "I'm afraid we have a big problem." What follows is a quote for a sum close to the national debt and a mechanic thinking about that trip to the Bahamas.

As he explains about the broken widget that jammed the "whatchamacallit," that caused the transmission to seize and the connecting rod to shatter, we haven't a clue what he is saying. But because we've known him for years, and he has done great work for us in the past, we say, "Ok, go ahead and fix it."

Do we really understand the physics, thermodynamics, mechanics, and electrical principles that make our vehicles dependable enough to entrust our lives too? Of course not, our confidence is based on nothing more than faith. As we trusted our mechanic, we also trust the engineers, technicians, and scientists that through hard work and experimentation have earned our confidence in their conclusions. We haven't personally verified their results, but through continuous dependable service and the testimony of others with the same experience, we accept their assurances of our safety. In other words, experience has taught us to trust completely. Even though our car broke down, we have concluded that the benefit is worth the risk. Perhaps we have just gotten lazy and complacent enough not to challenge the possibilities and to live in blind trust. In our defense, what else can we do?

What do we really know about the things that we have absolute confidence in every day of our lives or the people that we entrust with ourselves and our families? MacArthur says simply, "Faith is believing. You live by faith every day of your life. You turn on your faucet, fill the glass, and drink it. That's faith. You don't know what's really in that water. Faith is trusting. You go to a restaurant, and you eat what they serve you. We all live by faith. That's the only way we can survive."[21]

It seems to me that we place a tremendous faith in science yet reserving our commitment to the God who created us all because there is insufficient material proof.

I would challenge the notion that science deserves our trust more than Jesus Christ because science depends on empirical evidence. Even though the argument has grown tiresome because of its frequency, the repetition has not seemed to have changed people's minds. Science has proven itself to be dependable but only after years, decades, or even centuries of failure and false conclusions. I rarely accept a new theory or scientific discovery at face value for I know that only time will tell.

I don't know how many times natural science has changed and theorized about the origins of life before coming to the conclusion that the evolution of species is correct. They are still perfecting the theory as it seems to change with every difficulty encountered. It suggests to me that during the process of streamlining that more faith is necessary at each step. Throughout the whole process, "facts" seem to come and go, yet the presuppositions continue. Perhaps this proves as effectively as anything else that

---

[21.] John MacArthur, *The Wrath of God*, Moody Press ed, John MacArthur's Bible Studies (Chicago: Moody Press, 1986), 9.

faith plays as much a part in science as it does in theology if not more so. Like MacArthur says, "That's the only way we can survive."

Faith Encompasses a Large Part of Our Lives

Faith is as much part of our daily lives as conversation with friends and coworkers. We trust the foods we eat will help us and not kill us. We trust that the machines we use will perform as expected and the instruments that monitor them are giving us truth and not lie. We trust that the company we work for will stay in business long enough to pay us the agreed upon salary. We trust that the promises made to us will be fulfilled.

Faith is a comfort. It keeps us from worry and helps us to relieve our minds from overburdening detail. Faith is necessary for our peace of mind. All we have to do is decide for ourselves that something is worthy of our trust, and we can then put it out of our minds.

Faith, trust, belief, hope, and expectation are all words that basically refer to the same things. They apply in one degree or another to everything that we know. Faith is the emotional response to knowledge that gives us the will to commit ourselves to action. Wherever there is knowledge, there must be faith in its validity. Once the validity is accepted, we make the decision to act. This is what "will" is.

Realizing then that faith is such a common and important part of our minute-by-minute lives, we must decide what to have faith in. Obviously, decisions are the result of our knowledge and our confidence based on our own judgment of that knowledge. We have already seen how science can let us down. But many people disregard science leaving it to the scientists. These people may believe in a multitude of other things, probably chief on the list is finance.

Money can create a sense of security since money can resolve a lot of conflict. The problem, of course, is that the acquisition and retention of money is rarely under one person's control. With the value of things changing based on their supply, it can take more and more money to maintain the level of security hoped for. A house in one part of the country may cost twice as much in another part of the country. Things that we buy may become less valuable with use. Depreciation then eats up our security like rust on a new car. Governments come and go, and the requirements to maintain them will vary from administration to administration. Stocks rise and fall based upon the whim of investors.

Security from a large bank account is as fleeting as smoke on the wind. What good is a million dollars when a two-bedroom house on a 50×100 lot costs 1.1 million? When taxes take over half of earned income, it requires more and more to just breakeven. Rising medical costs can eat up a life's savings in one hospital stay. It is unreasonable to place all faith in money to make us happy and to keep us that way.

Others place their confidence in themselves: in their abilities, in their physical strength, in their care of their healthy bodies, in their position in life. I knew a man who had supreme confidence in his own intelligence. He was convinced that he could figure his way out of anything. While sitting in church one Sunday, his back began to ache. He shifted position in hopes that it would remove the strain on a tired muscle, but the pain persisted. As a matter of fact, it grew worse so he went to a quiet room and lay down. The pain grew worse, so he left and went home. His wife, who had worked all night, was still asleep. He awakened her, and she rushed him to the emergency room where he was diagnosed with cardiovascular disease that had caused a heart attack. He survived and was told that the damage was minimal. As time went on, however, he who had depended on his excellent memory and sharp mind, found himself unable to concentrate or remember details. He was diagnosed with depression resulting from trauma to his heart and small stroke that occurred at the same time. He spends his life now in anxiety because he's afraid what he thinks may not be true or that he has forgotten important details. People find this out and lie to him claiming he has forgotten what he agreed to. His confidence in his own judgment has been destroyed. Self-assurance is also false hope.

Faith placed in the things of the earth is disappointing. We find ourselves lost and disillusioned. Our trust must be firmly placed in a proven source. I would suggest that faith in God through Jesus Christ is no riskier than faith in the status quo of a man who has not known God at all.

In his book *The Case for Faith*, Lee Strobel posited eight questions he believed were the most common questions asked about God which created difficulty believing in Christianity. After he completed many interviews with those he considered to be experts, he says, "My conclusion is that Christianity emerged unscathed. After spending a year investigating 'The Big Eight' objections, I remained utterly convinced that the most rational and logical step people can take is to invest their faith in Jesus of Nazareth."[22]

To us that know Him, it is the only faith sensible. So how do we approach the problem? Can we just decide to believe? Yes, but is that good enough? It seems to me that merely believing in God is not sufficient. James tells us: "You believe that God is one. You do well; the demons also believe, and shudder" (James 2:19, NKJV). In other words, belief alone is no better than intellectual acknowledgment. As a matter of fact, such a faith is only on the surface. It involves no more than a change of mind. Faith must be a matter of deeper concern, not only of depth but

---

[22.] Lee Strobel, *The Case for Faith: A Journalist Investigates the Toughest Objections to Christianity* (Grand Rapids, Mich: ZondervanPublishingHouse, 2000), 253.

of the depth specified by the Lord God Himself. It must be sufficient to engage God on our behalf. This help must come on His terms not ours. Our faith must be of sufficient depth to satisfy Him. If we are willing to trust in God to work out what is best for us, it would seem that a mere "head" faith will not provide what we expect. Therefore, our faith has to be much deeper. These words reveal to us the truth about saving faith. It is not enough to believe in a superficial way. That is why Paul teaches several conditions for saving faith. The first is to "believe unto righteousness." Lewis says regarding saving faith,

> The other set were accused of saying, "Faith is all that matters. Sin away, my lad, and have a good time and Christ will see that it makes no difference in the end." The answer to that nonsense is that, if what you call your "faith" in Christ does not involve taking the slightest notice of what He says, then it is not Faith at all-not faith or trust In Him, but only intellectual acceptance of some theory about Him.[23]

It must be a belief that is strong enough to change our behavior. It is a belief that changes our entire system of determining right and wrong. Paul calls it "unto righteous-

---

[23.] Lewis, *Mere Christianity*. 130.

ness" (Romans 10:10). Any belief that is strong enough to change our lifestyle is deep indeed.

A man has a cardiac event, and his doctor tells him that he must change his life in order to live. He's got to cut out the salt and greasy foods. He's got to lose weight, take medication, and exercise regularly for the rest of his life. Only the most foolish among us would disregard our doctor's advice. Such a change evidences a deep faith in what the doctor has told us. Would we expect any less faith in the Lord Jesus Christ for the Father to grant to us eternal life?

The other condition requires a disregard of worldly thinking. This second condition requires us to step out of normal reality and delve into a murky world of no outside, empirical, scientific evidence. It's easy to disregard the "supernatural" TV shows and horror stories that have thrilled and amazed us all our lives. The fact is that they are so outside science and daily experience that you just can't take them seriously. Basically, that is one reason we can be entertained by them, they're just too fantastic to be true. That makes them safe and assures us that they can never happen. They have no value other than entertainment. Yet that is Paul's second condition for saving faith. We must truly believe that God the Father resurrected Jesus alive from the dead.

I remember witnessing to a young girl about her soul. I asked her if she could believe that Jesus was the Son of God.

She said, "Yes." I then asked her if she believed that she was disobedient to God in living outside of His commandments. She said, "Yes." I then asked her if she believed that Jesus died on the cross and God raised Him from the dead, alive? She raised her eyebrows and said, "Are you kidding?"

I said "No, not at all." She walked away thinking I was crazy.

Paul asks us not only to believe but to be willing to "confess" or "profess" publicly that Jesus rose from the dead. We not only have to believe but say so in front of other people like that young girl. That requires a deeper faith because even though there were hundreds of witnesses (by biblical and historical accounts), it is so far beyond the realm of normal understanding that we balk at the idea. This is the second condition of saving faith. There is no scientific evidence or any record in secular history of anything like it ever having occurred. It becomes a matter of faith and trust in God's Word and eyewitness testimony. Saving faith exceeds "head knowledge" by a long shot for an honest person.

Faith in the wrong thing is just as unacceptable. Jesus said: "I am the way, the truth, and the life. No man comes to the Father accept by Me" (John 14:6, NKJV). The only way to approach the Father in heaven successfully is through Jesus Christ; anything else merely disappoints, frustrates, and finally condemns.

Shifting Sand

Some people are very dear to me, and they followed a religious road which was man-created. This group, which they became involved in, had predicted the imminent return of Jesus Christ on a particular day many times throughout their history. It was that one of those days was to arrive very soon at that time.

Their faith, though commendable, was misguided. The day came and went without fulfillment. The tragedy was that these dear ones had sold all their possessions and mortgaged their retirement and gave it to their religious leadership in anticipation of that day. When called to account, the leadership smugly replied that they had been misinformed and such a prediction had never taken place. When asked to return the funds, they refused. Now those dear ones were looking at a bleak future, but the worst of the matter was their destroyed faith. Now they had no hope and were lost. They had taught their children who had grown up in the religion. All their deceased family members had now no hope in the resurrection because like my dear ones, they had built their houses upon the shifting sand of false hopes.

It was the ultimate act of betrayal. Certainly, if they had read their Bible, they would have known that only the Father knows the day or the hour of the Lord's return, and anyone who claims otherwise is a liar and a false prophet.

Such stories scare us to death. How can we be sure what is true, and what is a lie? Well, the answer unfortunately is not easy either. Truth is we can't know for sure like we know that 2 + 2 = 4, but how much do we really know that is as absolute? "Very little" would be my honest answer. That is why it's called "faith." But we can begin with the same logic that we used to describe how easily we place our faith in science and personal ability, finances, etc.

If we go to our auto and we start it one thousand times, we can be reasonably sure it will start on the one thousand and first. If our alarm clock has performed reliably for ten years, we may be comfortable with the odds that it will awaken us tomorrow even though there are no guarantees.

It is my hope that information that is five thousand-plus years old and has never been successfully proven wrong or inaccurate is worthy of our trust. I speak of the Bible. It claims inspiration of God. It is archeologically and historically proven. It has been trusted by Christians for two thousand years and has persisted. If my car had that track record, I'd never sell it.

So then, I am not afraid to recommend it to you as the ultimate source of truth and the path of salvation that God would have us to travel if we would be part of His family. In simpler terms, if you want God on your side, the Bible is the truth and worthy of your faith and the true way to knowledge of Him. It is trustworthy. Faith is stubborn determination not to relent. Once we have been convinced that our faith is well placed, we should not change our minds. That is called perseverance, and we will talk about that latter.

As we mentioned at the beginning, there is great confusion in the world about what is right and wrong. Many people, even Christians are like that old deacon that I mentioned before. They act upon whatever the situation seems to call for. Their standard for right and wrong changes as the situation becomes more complicated, uncomfortable, or difficult. Such an attitude is labeled situation ethics. The wonderful thing about the word of God is that it's not just dos and don'ts; it is principles for daily living. Those principles don't change with the wind. James said, "If any of you lacks wisdom, let him ask of God, who gives to all liberally and without reproach, and it will be given to him. But let him ask in faith, with no doubting, for he who doubts is like a wave of the sea driven and tossed by the wind. For let not that man suppose that he will receive anything from the Lord; he is a double-minded man, unstable in all his ways" (James 1:5–8, NKJV). Those who hold to situational ethics will find instability in their ways. If a decision is based on the easiest way, on what can he base his next decision on? When a fisherman wants to hold his boat in a current, he ties to a log or other obstruction. This works fine until he has to hold his boat in the middle of the river. Without an anchor staying over the fishing hole is tough. That's what God's truth is, an anchor in all situations.

As we grow, we find out that His word is a very trustworthy anchor. Our confidence in its stability makes us solid decision-makers. People begin to depend on our opinions and advice because the truth always tells.

The Good Fight of Faith

I would be remiss if I closed the chapter on faith without talking about the challenges Christian faith must face. If our enemy is strong and cunning and older than mankind, we know he must be a formidable adversary indeed. He will attempt every means at his disposal to trip us up, tempt us to sin, and otherwise destroy our faith.

When I was a young man entering college, my chosen major was biology. I, as a young Christian man, was fascinated by all living things and particularly the systems created by God for their mutual, beneficial interdependence. But as I began to study, I realized that everything I was being taught contradicted my faith. The idea that one animal arose through evolutionary processes from another totally different "kind" confused and bewildered me. Surely my parents, Sunday school teachers, pastors, and deacons could not be this wrong! But they were not as educated and worldly as my professors, were they? A great crisis of faith ensued, and I was led astray from the truth. It was years afterward and much suffering before I repented and came back to the Lord.

The enemy will find your weakness and attempt to exploit it. Paul commands Timothy, "Fight the good fight of faith, lay hold on eternal life, to which you were also called and have confessed the good confession in the presence of many witnesses" (1 Timothy 6:12, NKJV). Our fight is not with men but spiritual forces. Again, Paul says, "For we do not wrestle against flesh and blood, but against principalities, against powers, against the rulers of the darkness of this age, against spiritual hosts of wickedness in the heavenly places" (Ephesians 6:12, NKJV). But never forget, we do wrestle. The enemy and his helpers must be resisted. Your life depends on it. The assurance is that if we have peace with our Lord, He will fight for us, and if He is with us, who can resist Him? But if you permit it, sin will become the weakness in your armor. Do not give it place in your life, or it will become a stronghold of suffering and shame. The enemy will use it to create guilt and despair in your life, but God gives us the Word to tell us the truth. John tells us, "These things I have written to you who believe in the name of the Son of God, that you may know that you have eternal life, and that you may continue to believe in the name of the Son of God" (1 John 5:13, NKJV). This is the reason that John wrote the letter to his "children," to provide comfort, support, and assurance. Don't believe Satan's lies. Remember the Scripture, "Let your conduct be without covetousness; be content with such things as you have. For He Himself has said, 'I will never leave you nor forsake you.'" (Hebrews 13:5, NKJV).

The conundrum comes when Satan uses friends and family to trip you up. He has his followers, too, and not only demons but men and women as well. He will use all the glitter and glamor of the "beautiful people." The "in crowd" and the most popular and well liked of the world's crowd. Don't be fooled. God never tempts you to sin. Only Satan does that. However, we must remember that Christ died for them as well, so we must resist their influence but not with arrogance but humility. We must remember that like me, you can be swept away with their deceit as well. Do not burden yourself down with failure. "Therefore submit to God. Resist the devil and he will flee from you." (James 4:7, NKJV). One of the greatest pressures the enemy can bring is peer pressure. But we must present a strong Christian witness before these people. We must be "watchmen" on the tower, and we must do all we can to bring the truth to them so that perhaps they might be won or brought back to the Lord. It is a wondrous service to our Lord to win a soul or to turn someone to repentance and away from sin.

CHAPTER 8

Virtue

But now you yourselves are to put off all these: anger, wrath, malice, blasphemy, filthy language out of your mouth. Do not lie to one another, since you have put off the old man with his deeds, and have put on the new man who is renewed in knowledge according to the image of Him who created him, where there is neither Greek nor Jew, circumcised nor uncircumcised, barbarian, Scythian, slave nor free, but Christ is all and in all.

—Colossians 3:8–11, NKJV

Saving faith involves the Holy Spirit, bringing conviction to the heart of the seeker. The Lord says, "And when He has come, He will convict the world of sin, and of righteousness, and of judgment" (John 16:8, NKJV). In these passages, Jesus is referring to the Holy Spirit. His conviction reveals to us an understanding that we have never known before.

That understanding is our failure as individuals who are "good enough" and is revealed by the conviction of the Holy Spirit. He shows us the absolute certainty of the truth of God, a truth that is born into our very souls. It is a certainty of the matter that is virtually undeniable. It is knowledge of our unfitness to be in God's presence. All this is made available to us merely by believing and trusting its truth. Faith, then, is the gateway to salvation.

But there are many barriers that the seeker may need to confront and overcome before he breaks down and admits that he needs salvation. These are extremely subjective because the Holy Spirit brings to his mind his personal inadequacy or unworthiness for salvation.

According to John 16:8, The Holy Spirit brings conviction in three areas. All of these areas require a familiarity with virtue. The seeker must know right from wrong. He has to know that he is wrong and God is right. This requires some means of comparison. If everyone makes up their own standard, then no one is wrong. Romans 5:13 reminds us of the necessity of the law for conviction, "For, until the law sin was in the world, but sin is not imputed when there is no law." The word "imputed" here means "laid to account" or "held against someone."

The conviction that the Holy Spirit brings is the law. It may not be in the form of stone tablets, but it will be an assurance that past behavior has been wrong. This is the conviction of past sins as identified by the law. A person may not be able to quote the Ten Commandments, but the Holy Spirit will use them to reveal sin in a way that the seeker will recognize.

He may remember the time he lied to his mother; this would be bearing false witness. It may be the time he embezzled from a business partner; this would be stealing. He may have betrayed his wife; this would be adultery. His realization of these things would confirm in his mind and emotions that these acts were hated by God. He may even realize that God's judgment against these acts is death. He knows he is guilty and in need of forgiveness and mercy.

The Holy Spirit Convicts

The necessity of conviction is without question. Conviction comes from the recognition of good in contrast to evil and the implication that good is the correct choice. No matter what we think, the fact is that everything boils down to this simple choice. We choose to do the right thing in the midst of understanding what the wrong thing is. Essentially, this is the only choice that is available to men. The decision to choose right or wrong is a choice that comes from the conviction of God against our sin and the desire to be forgiven and joined into fellowship with Him. Sin breaks fellowship with our Heavenly Father.

In the newly repentant, born-again sinner, the attitude of the heart is to be Christlike. He chooses to be Christlike in the face of being selfish. Paul said, "Be imitators of me even as I am of Christ" (1 Corinthians 11:1)

It is only through repentance that virtue can be realized. Once the decision is made, even before the actions are taken, or the cognitive knowledge is accrued, a supernatural thing occurs in the soon-to-be-baby Christian. Many people want to call it a conscience or the new man, prevenient grace or other such synonyms, but the fact is that God the Holy Spirit guides and directs the thinking processes that allow new believers to make the right choices. He will know with uncommon certainty that this is a good thing to do. He will humble himself and confess to the Lord his need for forgiveness. He will ask the Lord to save him, and the Lord will immediately grant his request, and the newly born-again baby Christian will now know peace and the joy of forgiveness.

Now, when confronted with temptation his entire person will realize unease or disquiet in the framework of the peace of God within His soul. As he continues in his misunderstanding, the disquiet will increase to the point of distraction. If he chooses to disobey from willfulness, the unease may turn to physical discomfort. Through this process, he learns to obey even before he begins to study. It is a process that will continue until further maturity is reached.

To me, this is one of the most precious things that can happen in the life of the Christian. It provides so much assurance and increases our faith immensely. It brings to mind the sure and certain knowledge that the Lord Jesus Christ is truly with us. It affirms our faith by showing that He really loves us enough to correct our errors.

As a child, I knew that my dad loved me because he showed me things that could hurt me or cause me difficulty in my life. Often, I didn't realize it at the time, but reflection soon showed me the truth of it even when the instruction made me angry because I couldn't get what I wanted. Later, I was glad someone loved me enough to tell me the truth.

At this stage in the believer's development, the Lord is very gentle. Oh! What a treat it is to be admonished by a loving Heavenly Father. This precious correction soon makes the young believer hungry for more. Like a baby loves mother's milk, so the new Christian loves the close and personal attention he gets from the Father. Once again, good behavior is rewarded and wickedness is discouraged.

A strong motivation to please the Heavenly Father develops. We wish to do good so that this sweet connection will continue. Like a young child and his parents, the baby relationship is used to teach truth and establish new behaviors. Throughout our walk with Christ, this sweet relationship grows into fellowship and love and boldness in the faith.

In our pursuit of this fellowship, we learn to love the things that Jesus loves and to hate what He hates. The things that He hates are sin and particularly pride and willfulness. The things that He loves are humility and faith. We practice those things in our lives that will grow and strengthen the positive and weaken the negative. Paul calls this "Putting on the new man" (Ephesians 4:24, NKJV) and "Putting to death the deeds of the body" (Romans 8:13, NKJV).

Virtue then becomes a practice in which the flesh is denied and the "new man" who is created and controlled by the Holy Spirit is placed upon the "throne" of our will.

The word translated into our English for "virtue" also means power. In essence, our consciences are submitted to the will of God, not ourselves, and the Holy Spirit gives us virtue or power to comply with it.

Don't be confused. Righteousness is our standing before the law. We have been imputed the very righteousness of Christ Himself because of Justification. Therefore, we cannot be more righteous by our acts, attitude, or any choice at all that we can make. Righteousness is not based in us but in Christ.

Virtue, however, is a different matter. Virtue is moral excellence. It is choosing to do the right thing and realizing the power to do it. When all of our friends want us to participate in questionable or even sinful acts, the choice to be virtuous stops us, and the power of the Holy Spirit in us gives us the ability to do what we know the Lord would want us to do instead. His virtue becomes ours. His lifestyle becomes ours. His choices become ours. Living a virtuous life is a reflection of the power of Christ in us. A good tree yields good fruit, and a rotten tree yields rotten fruit. The greater our submission to Christ, the sweeter and more consistent our fruit will be. Virtue is a choice we make to honor our God and His Christ. Thomas A. Kempis writes regarding John 8:12, "These are the words of Christ, by which we are taught, how we ought to imitate his life and manners, if we will be truly enlightened, and be delivered from all blindness of heart. Let therefore our chief endeavor be, to meditate upon the life of Jesus Christ."[24]

Questionable Acts

This sinful world is full of opportunities to commit questionable acts. On the surface, these things may not be sinful, but on the other hand, they are just not conducive to a Christian life.

It's not easy to pinpoint these acts because they are subjective. They are almost entirely based on the individual and what the weakness of his or her flesh is. Some may have trouble with going to baseball games because of the beer drinking that goes on there, so they choose to watch it on TV with Christian brothers and sisters. Alcohol is one of the big question marks to Christians because there seems to

---

[24]. Kempis, Thomas A., *The Imitation of Christ*, Moody Paperback Edition 1984. Editor Paul M.Bechtel (Chicago: Moody Press, 1980), 23.

be a clash between Scripture and culture. Where the Bible does not specifically condemn alcohol consumption, it forbids drunkenness. Some Christians have no problem drawing the line, but others are less under control and will cross the line. Alcohol and recreational drugs are the scourge of modern society. Alcohol and drugs are implicated in an estimated 80 percent of offenses leading to incarceration in the United States such as domestic violence, driving while intoxicated, property offenses, drug offenses, and public-order offenses.[25] I abstain from the use of all non-prescribed, mood-altering substances so as not to damage my testimony (for my weaker brother's sake) or my ministry. Drunkenness, which includes drug abuse, is sin and forbidden by Scripture. One can't become addicted if one doesn't use it. Other practices, however, are not so cut and dried. Romans chapter 14 and 1 Cor 8:1–11 speak to questions of conscience and choosing to live with a Christian worldview that is largely defined by our understanding of the Scriptures and our own consciences.

In 1 Cor. 8:1–11, Paul talks about violating our consciences and reminds us that in any particular situation, we ourselves can either be the weak brother or the strong one. He uses the example of eating meat that has been previously offered to idols in the pagan temples. This food

---

[25]. Stephen Wilcox, "Alcohol, Drugs and Crime," accessed January 27, 2018, https://www.ncadd.org/about-addiction/alcohol-drugs-and-crime.

was sold in the marketplace in Corinth by the leadership of the worshippers of false gods to raise money. The meat was offered to the false gods, but if the meat was not consumed by the priests, it was sold at a reduced price and was generally very good quality. Some Christians at Corinth felt that to purchase such goods was to hinder the cause of Christ and to support pagan worship. They also felt that such food had been spiritually tainted and was unfit for Christian consumption. Paul told them not to violate their consciences. There was nothing sinful about the meat but to go against their conscience was. In Romans 14, he also warned them that others might not feel that way and could eat with freedom. Such persons should not be condemned by those conscientious objectors because only God can judge the heart for individual sin. Denying the conscience violates it, and people who do this become petty, carnal, and judgmental. Romans 14 and 1 Corinthians 8 are very similar. A comparison of these two passages can be very helpful in doubtful matters.

Carnality in Christianity

One of the saddest qualities of a carnal Christian is his continued denial of what his conscience tells him is no good for him. As time goes on and he continues this denial, he disregards his conscience until it is no longer heard. He is then described as "Having his conscience seared with a hot iron." As this process continues, he becomes desensitized to the urgings of the Holy Spirit. In giving himself over to his own desires, he becomes less and less aware of his spiritual surroundings. An old song lyrics describes it to a tee, "I've been down so long, I forget what up looks like." These people soon begin to look at the world with sensual eyes. Decisions become based on feelings such as pride, lust, and self-satisfaction and not reason and charity. They become the source of irritation and strife within the church because they have become blinded to the ways of God and the Holy Spirit. They are always the dissenters in the business meetings and would rather confront than endure. The counsel of faithful Christians becomes foolishness to them and sometimes insulting.

With the denial of the conviction of the Holy Spirit to temper their emotions, their anger rises and flashes out. Making their point is more important than peace. A lot of churches have been broken by such outbursts of choler. They have been manipulated by Satan, and they don't even know it. The faithful bow their heads and pray that God will reveal to them the truth and bring them to repentance.

They become like the woman with green hair who doesn't realize how pitiful she looks to others. No matter what church you align yourself with, these people will always be there. The faces will change, but the same qualities will be seen. Some will repent, and God will bring them back. When that happens, we must welcome them because we, ourselves, can be tempted to fall as well but most of all, because God commands it.

But in most cases, the pride will be out of control at this point, and they will loathe to admit their wrong and will leave. It has been this way from the beginning of the church. Some years later, a new pastor or deacon will come along and start going through the old church role and find their names, a sad legacy to carnality and pride. Many churches have taken to removing names from the active membership role or removing them altogether.

Virtue is the quality that allows people to live in humility, truth, and peace. It is a constant reminder that God's way is the right way. It requires submission to the will of God and a realization that without Him, we are foolish prey awaiting slaughter. Pride and willfulness become abhorrent in us and in others.

There is a trap that awaits us though. We find ourselves becoming judgmental and gradually more intolerant when we see others indulging themselves while we deny ourselves. Our walk of virtue becomes self-righteousness and pride. This is another manifestation of carnality. One of the things that keeps us in perspective is our growing in knowledge of Jesus Christ and His loving kindness. Knowledge comes in different ways, but study of the Scripture is the most reliable.

• CHAPTER •

9

Knowledge

As faith grows, also grows with it—uncertainty. Many questions begin to arise in the mind of the new believer. A need to understand more begins to develop. It is a gnawing question that evolves from the things he sees in his life as well as in the lives of others. Why do I keep having trouble with the same old sin? Why is God so loving, yet I see so much trouble in the world? How can I let God be a bigger part of my life? What can I do to fulfill His will in my life? What does God have in mind for me? Who should I marry?

All these questions and thousands more just like them begin to invade his thinking. Pretty soon, he is so distracted he no longer feels at ease. It's as if there is unrepentant sin going on, yet nothing comes to mind. Based on the sweet and gentle unction of the Holy Spirit in the recent past, he becomes more concerned. Always after such struggle in his soul, the Holy Spirit shows the sin and the proper actions to take to repair it. But this time is different. There are no leanings toward repentance, only a call for unspecified action. A baby Christian will then seek the advice of an older Christian, perhaps a pastor.

When he explains to the pastor, the pastor will smile internally as he knows that the Holy Spirit is teaching this baby some very basic lessons. His joy will leap up as he watches what the Holy Spirit does. He will advise the young Christian that perhaps the Holy Spirit is urging him to "get plugged in" to a congregation of born-again, spirit-filled believers where he can see God in others and more clearly in himself.

Maybe he will ask when his salvation experience occurred. The next question will help the pastor to formulate a growth-assistance plan for the new Christian. "Has anyone spoken to you about baptism?" He may ask and then explain how baptism is the next step in obedience. Further, he may mention that growth may not continue until, in obedience, this simplest of all basic ordinances is accomplished. He will show the new Christian the Great Commission verses and tell him that the Bible has all of the answers needed. He might ask a mature Christian in the congregation to disciple the new believer and make the contact arrangements.

The new Christian has now been introduced to the source of knowledge that every Christian needs—personal, spiritual, guidance. With Baptism accomplished, a whole new vista of information is opened up. The Holy Spirit now takes the new Christian and plugs him into the world of other Christian believers, the visible church. He begins to move him into the paths of other Christian men and women who exemplify the things he reads in Scripture.

The Pursuit of Knowledge

Harold Mare says regarding first Corinthians 8:3, "With the essential ingredient of love, knowledge is tempered and made the right kind of discerning and compassionate knowledge exhibited when one loves God. In loving God, a person shows that he is known by God—that God recognizes him as his own and as having the right kind of knowledge, because he is exercising it in love to his fellow Christians and to God."[26]

Knowledge is a thing, like love, that has many interpretations depending upon perspective. It may be information that comes in written form. It can also be information that is received through the senses. However, at this point it must be clear that God has revealed Himself to us in a convincing and personal way. By this, I mean prior to any factual evidence. He has shown Himself and His righteous-

---

[26.] Frank E. Gaebelein, ed., *The Expositor's Bible Commentary: With the New Internat. Version of the Holy Bible; in 12 Vol. 10: Romans - Galatians*, 19. print. (Grand Rapids, Mich: Regency Reference Libr, 19), 239.

ness to us through the power and illumination of His Holy Spirit. For me to suggest that I have come to the knowledge of God by an act of my own will is self-delusional. What would lead me to the conclusion that I am imperfect if I have no evidence to condemn myself that I am wrong? If I am my only judge, it is only natural to assume that I am right and all other possibilities are wrong. Given the selfish nature of the human spirit, this is the ultimate rational conclusion, yet no one claims to be perfect.

Knowledge of this nature then must come from outside ourselves. Once again, proof of God's intervention into our personal lives is laid out for those with eyes to see.

As simple human beings, we find ourselves asking ever-increasing questions both in number and complexity. The sad part is that we rarely come to the right conclusions on our own. How did Cain get his wife? How could God have created light before creating the sun? Why did God choose Abel over Cain? Why all these questions and no clear explanation? Entire religions have been created by misguided conclusions from searches for knowledge. Solomon said, "For in much wisdom is much grief, and he who increases knowledge increases sorrow" (Ecclesiastes 1:18, NKJV).

If we continue asking these kinds of questions, the true searcher will start digging into all the resources he can to find an answer. It becomes a strong incentive to learn. Many people have come to peace by digging for the answers to impossible questions. As we search and pray for guidance, we begin finding answers to other questions not directly related to what we're looking into. The search itself, sometimes (perhaps most of the time) yields unexpected rewards and in itself becomes satisfying. Isn't God wonderful?

The Nature of Knowledge

There are all kinds of knowledge. Basically, knowledge in itself is just a gathering of facts and data. But knowledge is more complicated than just gathering data. It involves experience and cognizance.

Knowledge tends to be much more informative and helpful when it incorporates emotion and reason. It tends to cut through all the filters that the mind uses to try and sort things out. The things we know come not only from raw data but from observation and experimentation to determine truth. What we are basically referring to is information. Information is facts and data from which we garner knowledge. It starts off with the certainty of ignorance. We know that we are ignorant and need to be educated in order to grow in the grace of God. We need to understand what God's plan is and how we fit in.

But information without truth is nothing. Truth is the foundation that makes information effective and useful. Worldly knowledge does not always include truth. True information comes from years, even decades, of gathering data and eliminating disinformation and lies and avoiding preconception and deception. How many centuries did it take to figure out that the world was round and orbited the sun? We have an entire age in our history in which the truth was obscured by religious dogma and pure stubbornness. Galileo proved beyond doubt that the earth was not the center of the universe but orbited the sun. He was tormented and hounded through most of his life because such ideas contradicted prevailing thought.

Medicine was severely hampered in its search for the truth because certain powerful authorities believed dissection of the human body to be sinful. As a result, millions died horribly during the plague-ridden Dark Ages.

Information without truth is not real. It is only when information is true that we have the tools in which to use our will to alter our lives in conformity to God's plan. Until then, we are like ships without a compass. We have the power to accomplish our journey but not the means for navigation. We have nothing to direct us. This is why the Holy Spirit will "drive" us to search. When Jesus was beginning His work on the earth, the Holy Spirit "drove" (AV) Him into the wilderness. There He fasted and prayed for forty days before being tempted by Satan to take shortcuts. If He (the Holy Spirit) drove Jesus, it should come as no surprise that He will also drive us. I am certain that being "driven" was not a pleasant experience for the Lord. Neither is it for us. Many times, the Lord will push us against the limits of our comfort zones to prepare us for, and direct us toward, the knowledge that we need. Trust Him.

The Trustworthy Compass

A difficulty arises when we search for the truth. All kinds of well-intentioned advice come rolling in. When I was a young man, an older member of the congregation gave me some very good advice. He said, "Always set aside a tenth of your income for God cause if you don't, He will take it anyway." I look back on that and chuckle because he was such a hard-nosed old soul. However, the same man told me at a different time, "Church is church but business is business." He chose to live with two worldviews: the business man on the one hand who had a different moral compass and the deacon on the other with another set of rules. Conflict between the two was inevitable. Even as a young man, I remembered what Jesus had said I had read in scripture, "No one can serve two masters; for either he will hate the one and love the other, or else he will be loyal to the one and despise the other. You cannot serve God and mammon" (Matthew 6:24, NKJV). Scripture will always steer you right. So I learned a valuable lesson. Even a good apple tree matures apples at different rates. Some are ready to eat, and some are green and to be rejected until ready. Advice is no different.

The Scripture is always the better choice when it comes to wisdom. But few things come easily and without difficulties. The Bible is no different. Learning to study it effectively is not easy. It takes some work. Even though the words and meanings are dependable, infallible, and proven over the centuries, our understanding is not. Therein lies the rub.

One of the best ways to aid understanding is to ask someone that you trust for the meaning. Your pastor is one of the best sources. Another is the published opinions of others who are of your belief system, notably commentaries. When word meanings are difficult because the words are unfamiliar or archaic, a bible dictionary is helpful.

The Scriptures are made of different kinds of literature. There is history and epistles or personal letters. There is poetry and wisdom literature. All of these types may make the meanings difficult to interpret. A set of bible maps is very helpful when studying history. Also, secular books on world history can help put things into perspective.

Just as each person has a different perspective on the events witnessed by a number of people so the Gospels may present different viewpoints of the life of Jesus. Each author has events, lifestyle, culture, and social position which have influenced the way he perceives events. Luke was a physician, so his description of the Lord's crucifixion is more physical and perhaps medical than Matthew's. All these things are just drops in the ocean of information available.

But one thing is certain. There is nothing in the Scripture that was not inspired, permitted, and preserved by the Lord God Himself. "All Scripture is given by inspiration of God and is profitable for doctrine, for reproof, for correction, for instruction in righteousness" (2 Timothy 3:16, NKJV).

But what help is there if God shows us the right way and we turn our backs on it. If we decide to follow Jesus, we must determine in our own minds to do the things that we understand that He wants us to do. That means commitment, bravery, and self-control.

CHAPTER 10

Self-Control

Enter by the narrow gate; for wide is the gate and broad is the way that leads to destruction, and there are many who go in by it. Because narrow is the gate and difficult is the way which leads to life, and there are few who find it.
—Matthew 7:13–14, NKJV

Now is the time when the new Christian begins to understand what Jesus meant when He referred to the "narrow gate" and the "straight way." The Christian walk asks the Christian to be Christlike. This requires us to be restrictive in our choices. Indulgence is a word that defines the old man and his lifestyle, not the new, born-again Christian. If I am to be Christlike, I must deny myself and live for Him. That means making righteous choices. These choices involve volition or willpower. One of the primary virtues that marks a growing, maturing Christian is the power to say "No."

When the baby Christian first encountered sin, the Holy Spirit urged him to run away from it. Now armed with the knowledge that comes from the Scripture, he finds the Holy Spirit guiding him to Scripture. The Scripture teaches him not only to "flee youthful lusts" (2 Timothy 2:22) but to choose life directions that avoid temptation. He sees that certain situations and circumstances will lead him into places where he must choose righteousness over worldliness. Many times, his choices will determine his temptations. Temptations bring lust, and when lust is conceived, it brings sin. Resisting temptation is one way in which the Christian evidences self-control.

> Blessed is the man who endures temptation; for when he has been approved, he will receive the crown of life which the Lord has promised to those who love Him. Let no one say when he is tempted, "I am tempted by God"; for God cannot be tempted by evil, nor does He Himself tempt anyone. But each one is tempted when he is drawn away by his own desires and enticed. Then, when desire has conceived, it gives birth to sin; and sin, when it is full-grown, brings forth death. (James 1:12–15, NKJV)

One of the fruits of the Holy Spirit as listed in Galatians 5:23 is self-control. The fruits of the Spirit are listed after Paul tells us the "deeds of the flesh." From this, it is easy to see that the fruits of the Spirit are a guard against the acts of the flesh. So then, self-control or self-mastery can also be thought of as self-discipline under the control and with the help of the Holy Spirit.

It may be that this process up to this point has taken days, months, or even years. But the young Christian will soon learn that there are some things beyond his/her ability to do. What is the answer?

Prayer is the Answer to the Question

As always, God is the answer. He is ready, willing, and most importantly able. Prayer is the key to heavenly help. It is the door to miracles. God wants His children to ask because He loves to answer.

So the young Christian will ask, "How do I pray?"

"Well, you knew how to ask for forgiveness of sin, didn't you?", we might ask. And then young Christian will start getting a clue. He may have cried out, "Lord help me!" but may not have realized that this was a prayer. He may have said, "Thank you Lord" which is also a prayer. But the understanding that every concern or plea for help or even just going about your daily routine can be an occasion for prayer comes more slowly. Prayer is a personal conversation with God. It is sitting down and talking to our Lord person to person. It is praise, thankfulness, supplication, intercession, provision, and worship (After all, He is the revered and awesome God of creation). I pray for people as I pass them in the hallways; that would be intercession. I pray God will protect me on the highway; that is supplication. I ask God to bless my food and thank Him for it; that would be thankfulness for provision. I ask Him to watch over my family as they go through their day. But when I really need to talk without distraction to the Lord, I go somewhere private. He tells us in Matthew,

> And when you pray, you shall not be like the hypocrites. For they love to pray standing in the synagogues and on the corners of the streets, that they may be seen by men. Assuredly, I say to you, they have their reward. But you, when you pray, go into your room, and when you have shut your door, pray to your Father who is in the secret place; and your Father who sees in secret will reward you openly. And when you pray, do not use vain repetitions as the heathen do. For they think that they will be heard for their many words. Therefore do not be like them. For your Father knows the things you have need

of before you ask Him. In this manner, therefore, pray:

Our Father in heaven, Hallowed be Your name. Your kingdom come. Your will be done On earth as it is in heaven. Give us this day our daily bread. And forgive us our debts, As we forgive our debtors. And do not lead us into temptation, But deliver us from the evil one. For Yours is the kingdom and the power and the glory forever. Amen.

For if you forgive men their trespasses, your heavenly Father will also forgive you. But if you do not forgive men their trespasses, neither will your Father forgive your trespasses." (Matthew 6:5–15, NKJV)

An important point that many people gloss over is verses 14–15 which are the last two verses. Forgiveness of others is a necessity for God's forgiveness of us. God, because of His great love, has forgiven our huge and terrible debt of sin. He has given us a wonderful example to follow. What would be His response after forgiving us if we refuse to forgive others? I shudder to think. If the young Christian would be forgiven for the things he cannot fix, should he not equally forgive those who have hurt him?

Yes, of course. David Jeremiah says, "In your prayer each day you can build the foundation of a forgiving spirit even before you have been injured. You can ask God to help you each day to see the incredible debt He has paid on your behalf. You can ask Him to help you imitate the sacrificial love that cost Him so dearly."[27] When our hearts are broken, we cry out to the Father. When a dear friend is in trouble, we call out to the Father for them. But also, when our enemy suffers, we can intercede on their behalf and thereby evidence to God and ourselves that we forgive. Jesus said, "But I say to you, love your enemies, bless those who curse you, do good to those who hate you, and pray for those who spitefully use you and persecute you" (Matthew 5:44, NKJV).

Prayer will help us to understand God's will for our life. "For this reason we also, since the day we heard it, do not cease to pray for you, and to ask that you may be filled with the knowledge of His will in all wisdom and spiritual understanding" (Colossians 1:9, NKJV). As Peter desires our spiritual growth in the knowledge of Jesus Christ so does Paul. The necessity of prayer for knowledge of God's will for us is beyond question.

Another aspect of our prayer life helps us deal with the effects of government in our lives. No doubt, the govern-

---

[27]. Jeremiah, David P., *Prayer: The Great Adventure* (Sisters, Or.: Multnomah Publishers, 2004), 149.

ment can make our lives impossible or in the least, uncertain. The Bible tells us,

> Therefore I exhort first of all that supplications, prayers, intercessions, and giving of thanks be made for all men, for kings and all who are in authority, that we may lead a quiet and peaceable life in all godliness and reverence. For this is good and acceptable in the sight of God our Savior, who desires all men to be saved and to come to the knowledge of the truth." (1 Timothy 2:1–4, NKJV)

If we ask, the Lord will step in and change people's minds. He brings circumstances into the life of the King just as He does in our life. Remember, God loves to answer our prayers.

I cannot stress the importance of regular, heartfelt, faithful, and consistent prayer. As James tells us, "Confess your trespasses to one another, and pray for one another, that you may be healed. The effective, fervent prayer of a righteous man avails much" (James 5:16, NKJV).

It must be obvious that prayer is a huge part of our Christian life. It is proof that we are sanctified from the world. We have the privilege of coming to God on a personal basis. As the writer of Hebrews says, "For we do not have a High Priest who cannot sympathize with our weaknesses, but was in all points tempted as we are, yet without sin. Let us therefore come boldly to the throne of grace, that we may obtain mercy and find grace to help in time of need" (Hebrews 4:15–16, NKJV).

Willpower: Doing the Tough Stuff

When Joseph was sold into slavery by his brethren, he ended up in the house of Potiphar. He had no choice in the matter and was soon confronted with sin (Genesis 39). He was constantly bombarded with the opportunity to sin by the wife of Potiphar who relentlessly pursued him. Consistently, he rejected her advances for the sake of his respect for Potiphar and his reverence for the commandment of God.

Sometimes life pushes us into situations that are unavoidable and so it was with Joseph. He knew right from wrong and refused the attention of Potiphar's wife. Her anger at his rejection led her to accuse him to her husband out of scorn even though he was innocent. The false accusations landed him in prison. God, however, knowing all things, eventually rescued him and blessed him with greatness. Imagine all the things that must have gone through his head in the years till his release. Joseph is a wonderful example for a Christian who has to live in a world where sin and sinful persons have control.

It's tough to do the right thing when you know that it's going to make things more difficult. Joseph knew all too well the consequences of living in an unrighteous world. But as long as the world is full of unrighteousness, we should not expect justice or fairness from it at all.

It would be so easy to lie on your taxes to save a little money, after all, no one would know. The world and its system are greatly influenced by the wicked One. He uses every trick in the book to get us to make mistakes. He throws roadblocks in our way to trip us up and make us stumble. And when he does, he wants everyone that may be uncertain about salvation to witness it. The good news is that Jesus has beaten him and his world system of trickery (John 16: 33). (This would be a good place to use one of those imprecatory prayers.) Self-control as a function of willpower helps us to achieve the victory. "Be sober, be vigilant; because your adversary the devil walks about like a roaring lion, seeking whom he may devour" (1 Peter 5:8, NKJV). Prayers of supplication bring the power of the Savior to our aid. He is ready willing and able to help.

The world is constantly bombarding us with easy but sinful decisions. The Christian, just like Joseph, must live under a code of virtue which does not change based on the situation. It is a morality that is based in the pursuit of the scriptural virtues that we are discussing now. Almost always, if a thing is evil in one set of circumstances, it will be evil in another. Our ethics cannot change based upon the convenience or the consequences. Joseph found this out all too well. Knowing the truth and holding it dear, will always keep our feet planted in reality but in opposition to the world. It's easier to bend the rules rather than follow them, but when we violate our consciences, there is a spiritual price to pay. The Scripture says, "Therefore, to him who knows to do good and does not do it, to him it is sin" (James 4:17, NKJV).

Every year people make New Year's pledges. "I pledge to lose weight" or "I'm going to quit smoking" and the list goes on and on. The truth is that few people actually follow through to completion. Many students begin their college careers out of high school but half of them will not make it to the third year and will carry student loans on their backs for years having accomplished nothing. "After averaging together all one thousand responses, we found that when the average college dropout finally gave up on college, they owed $13,929.65 in student loan debt."[28] It's all a matter of willpower. Little choices sometimes create the biggest consequences. "Catch us the foxes, the little foxes that spoil the vines, for our vines have tender grapes" (Song of Solomon 2:15, NKJV).

Turning off the TV to study for tomorrow's classes. Staying home with your family instead of going out with

---

[28]. Mike Brown, "College Dropouts and Student Debt," *LendEDU* (blog), November 2, 2017, https://lendedu.com/blog/college-dropouts-student-loan-debt/.

your buddies. Willpower is our willingness to pursue a goal and stick to it to completion. It is also a distinctive part of our Christian walk.

No matter where we go or what we do, we always carry the fleshly, old man around with us. He is a part of who we are, having been born sons of Adam and daughters of Eve. He constantly cries out for satisfaction, and of course, such satisfaction is against God's plan for us. The flesh craves the things of this world, not those things above. The Christian walk becomes at times a battle between our flesh and our consciences. But the hope for victory lies in the "great and precious promises" as Peter says,

> Grace and peace be multiplied to you in the knowledge of God and of Jesus our Lord, as His divine power has given to us all things that pertain to life and godliness, through the knowledge of Him who called us by glory and virtue, by which have been given to us exceedingly great and precious promises, that through these you may be partakers of the divine nature, having escaped the corruption that is in the world through lust." (2 Peter 1:2–4, NKJV)

Living in a Fallen World

When the Christian begins to realize that there are places and things and even people that can create temptation to step back into the old lifestyle, he begins to exercise self-control. He avoids those things which call to him for wickedness. The old things that once brought pleasure now bring conviction. The realization that these are the things for which Jesus hung on the cross on our behalf brings a strong desire to resist and not disappoint the Savior. This is what Jesus meant when He said, "And lead us not into temptation, but deliver us from evil." Also, the Holy Spirit brings to bear the new desires and the rejection of the old hungers and passions. It is in this frame of mind that a young Christian can resist temptation, succeed and not be self-righteous because it is all because of Jesus and none of it is to Christian's credit.

In a world where the temptation to sin is all around us, the skill to resist requires practice, prayer, and sensitivity to the leading of the Holy Spirit. Where before, avoiding situations came from our own conscious choices, now the Holy Spirit leads us away from places of temptation in ways of which we may not even be aware. Of course, practice means to keep at it even when we fail. It is unrealistic and hypocritical to suggest that new Christians will live without sin, especially when mature Christians don't. But as we get older spiritually, we can help by offering encouragement, experience, and comfort when others fall, knowing that we, ourselves, are likely to stumble as well, no matter how old or mature we have become. We must remember how we felt when we made mistakes and how we wanted to be treated by those we looked up to, remembering the grace that the Lord showed and continues to show us.

Since probably the most powerful temptation that Christians face is lust of the flesh (1 John 2: 15–17) and primarily sexual desire, the Scriptures are perhaps louder about it than any other kind of sin. In Galatians we read, "I say then: Walk in the Spirit, and you shall not fulfill the lust of the flesh" (Galatians 5:16, NKJV). With worldly temptations to lust of the flesh greater now than ever before, it has become harder and harder to just say "No."

But there is another sin that results from a failure of self-control which is terribly dangerous, grievous, and long-term. It is unforgiveness. Anger and depression caused by spiritual problems come from the inability to control what happens around us. Joseph who is such a wonderful example of self-control must have known great frustration at Potiphar and his wife. Can you imagine the anger Joseph must have felt at having been treated so unfairly, especially after being innocent?

The result of unforgiveness is bitterness, and it is spiritual cancer. Self-control in this situation means letting go of the anger, the cause of which you can do nothing about.

It means forcing your mind to disregard pride and asking God to deal with it for you. It takes great self-control not to lash out in self-righteous indignation saying, "I am entitled, it is my right to seek vengeance." But God tells us, "Beloved, do not avenge yourselves, but rather give place to wrath; for it is written, 'Vengeance is Mine, I will repay,' says the Lord" (Romans 12:19, NKJV). Christians must realize that all judgment and subsequent punishment belongs to the Lord and none to us (Matthew 28:18, NKJV). We as Christians have no "rights" in the eyes of God. We are all guilty and deserving of judgment. What "right" do I have to decide another man's fate? As the Scripture says,

> If we say that we have no sin, we deceive ourselves, and the truth is not in us. If we confess our sins, He is faithful and just to forgive us our sins and to cleanse us from all unrighteousness. If we say that we have not sinned, we make Him a liar, and His word is not in us. (1 John 1:8–10, NKJV)

The development of self-control involves self-discipline. Discipline is what a young student learns when he sits down in the evening to do homework and study for the next day's lesson. Discipline is also a life skill. It keeps us from eating too much, from staying up late at night when we should be sleeping. It forces us to keep ourselves clean and our domestic chores completed. It helps us to watch our spending and keep track of our records. Self-discipline is a life skill that helps a young Christian as well. He begins to develop new habits and daily routines that encourage spirituality and submission to the Holy Spirit.

Self-Control and the Power of the Holy Spirit

The young Christian begins to get an idea about what the Christian walk is all about when he first tries to resist temptation by simply choosing to. The flesh gets stronger and stronger like a volume control that is inexorably being raised to an infinite level. The harder young Christian pushes, the harder his flesh pushes back. (See Romans 7). He will undoubtedly lose because he cannot resist the temptation in his flesh; he is too weak, and the flesh is too powerful. This in essence is the failure of the law. All it can do is condemn us for our failure but offer no path for success. The law screams "guilty" as loudly as possible in our soul then judges us for our inadequacy. It acts like an amplifier in an attempt at making our determination greater and our resolve more resolute by making our sin seem intensely sinful. Yet all it does is make our sin louder and our guilt greater. The Lord knows this but keeps telling us to resist. "Be ye Holy for I am Holy" (Leviticus 11:45).

Before Pentecost, the Jews fought this battle every moment of their lives. Can you imagine the faith it would take to continue fighting the battle after losing over and over again? How discouraging it must have been. But through it all, the Father told them He loved them, and if they persisted to the end, He would reward them with eternal life. Faith, faith, and more faith were necessary for them and is for us as well.

They looked harder and harder at the law trying to find ways to shield themselves from temptation. The Rabbis built spiritual walls around spiritual walls to shield themselves, not only from sin but from the possibility of the temptation to sin. As this process continued on, the walls themselves became the Law (Talmud), and the degree of compliance became horribly detailed. Around 400 BC, the Jews had become so idolatrous and unfaithful that a group of pious zealots arose and began to preach the severest of repentance. They had learned the hard lessons of the captivity and would push against apostasy, idolatry, and unrighteousness with all of their mind, spirit, and soul. They would call themselves "Pharisees." They would be so harsh that even minor successes against temptation would become boundless victories and the sources of the thing God hates the most, pride. Their pride and self-righteousness led them to mercilessness against those who failed.

Forgiveness was supplanted by harsher and harsher judgment. Just like Islamic fundamentalism, their desire to do good became an abomination twisting the holiness of God into an excuse to impose their will on the populace.

And because their self-sacrifices for the sake of self-righteousness seemed to accomplish God's command to honor, they would appoint themselves judge and jury over every person they came into contact with, judging this one righteous or that one a sinner and doing it with a clear conscience. They would accuse and punish with impunity. They could even justify and encourage vigilante mobs. The woman caught in adultery is a biblical account of such an incident (see John 8ff). And for all of the self-righteousness, Jesus called them hypocrites and servants of Satan. He even told the people "Do as the Pharisees say, but not as they do." Jesus said they were "as graves that appear not." Their attempts at self-control would lead to extreme self-righteousness and unjustified self-delusional pride.

However, the Christian has a "Helper" that the ancient Hebrews did not have. They were plagued by the law, righteous and holy as it was, with the constant bombardment of the flesh to sin. The ancients created rules and regulations to avoid temptation. This is probably the only way to deal with failure that is in our own power. The idea was to avoid every situation possible to eliminate the fleshly power and the certainty of failure. As a result, the Pharisees would treat anyone whom they deemed a "sinner" with disdain and rejection. They could rarely bring someone to repentance in any permanent way. They had no ministry of reconciliation, only condemnation and judgment. People avoided them like lepers.

But when the Lord was crucified and resurrected, everything changed. People's faith increased as eyewitness accounts began to surface. At the time of His resurrection, many of the dead came out of their graves and walked around Jerusalem! (Matthew 27:52–53). The disciples themselves were filled with confidence as their faith compounded again and again because they knew that everything Jesus preached was true and coming to pass before their eyes. Also, there was the assurance that all of His promises that had not yet come true undoubtedly would. The greatest of these would be the coming of the "Helper," the Holy Spirit, the "earnest of our salvation."

At Pentecost, after His resurrection, the disciples met in the upper room of an inn, and Jesus appeared to them through locked doors. He breathed on them and flaming tongues of fire appeared above their heads, and they manifested great feats of spiritual power. The greatest of these was not the most spectacular to see but was the most significant in daily living. Not only did the great increase in their faith give them confidence beyond anything they had ever known before, but their very nature changed.

Now when in the privacy of their own thoughts evil was pondered, a different emotional and physical reaction occurred. The very thoughts of the flesh were sickening and revolting in the worst way. The appeal was like something dead for days in the hot sun. It was not tolerable to continue. This is the reaction of the new creation to sin. It is the result of the "new birth" brought about by the promised "Indwelling Holy Spirit" who is given to every newborn Christian at conversion and promised by Jeremiah the Prophet. It was not immediate for the disciples like it is for us because Jesus "had not yet ascended" but after Pentecost, it was like a whole new world opened for them. Anderson tells us, "Before we received Christ, we were slaves to sin. Now because of Christ's work on the cross, sin's power over us has been broken."[29]

The compulsion to sin and its ability to compound endlessly facilitating our failure to live holy lives, otherwise known as the bondage of sin, had been broken forever. It is called the New Covenant or New Testament. We are no longer slaves to sin, but Christ has set us free. We are at liberty to serve and worship and resist sin successfully. And when we fail, as a result of the old sinful nature that is still a part of who we are, the Blood of Jesus Christ continually washes and cleanses our souls as a hot shower cleanses our bodies. "But if we walk in the light as He is in the light, we have fellowship with one another, and the blood of Jesus Christ His Son cleanses us from all sin" (1 John 1:7, NKJV). Daily prayer and Bible study keep the Holy Spirit at the forefront of our consciences and clear in our ears as we go about our daily lives. The greater our ability

---

[29.] Neil T. Anderson, *The Bondage Breaker*, Updated and expanded (Eugene, Or: Harvest House, 2000), 11

to communicate with the Lord, the better our ability to live Christlike in a selfish world.

These things all require self-discipline, but the primary sin that seems most to be affiliated with the virtue of self-control is the lust of the flesh, chastity specifically. All of the things that tempt us in our bodies seem to be the most in opposition to self-control. And, of course, chief among these in an adult is sexual immorality.

Dealing with Immorality

Arguably, the most prolific sin visible in the modern world is immorality. Yet it is one of the least discussed because it resides in the most personal and least controllable areas of our lives. When the Lord tells a young man to "flee" youthful lust, it is because he cannot stand against it alone. The temptation to live immorally has always been one of the main reasons for the downfall of many of God's men and women.

King David was particularly plagued by this sin. His lust for Bathsheba led to murder and the death of a newborn son. The sin showed up in his children as well. It led to incest, rape, usurpation of his throne, war, and death. Solomon, David's second son by Bathsheba, became an apostate (one who rejects God and His ways).

The Bible says that Solomon's wives led him away from God. "For it was so, when Solomon was old, that his wives turned his heart after other gods; and his heart was not loyal to the Lord his God, as was the heart of his father David" (1 Kings 11:4, NKJV). God was greatly displeased. "So, the Lord became angry with Solomon, because his heart had turned from the Lord God of Israel, who had appeared to him twice" (1 Kings 11:9, NKJV).

The story of King David's failure begins in 2 Samuel 11. David sees Bathsheba, the wife of Uriah the Hittite, bathing on her rooftop. He begins to lust after her (notice this begins with voyeurism). Her husband is away, and David sends for her and has relations with her. When she becomes pregnant, David concocts a scheme to cover their shame and betrayal. He sends for her husband, Uriah, under a pretense of reporting on the war's progress in order to allow Uriah to lay with his wife. The subterfuge (lie) was intended to convince everyone that Uriah was the father. Uriah, however, was an honorable man and would not avail himself of the comforts of home while everyone else endured the hardships of the campaign.

As sin often does, the consequences became compounded when David plots to remove Uriah from the picture by orchestrating his murder in battle. Immorality has now progressed to murder, and the Lord God of Heaven has had enough.

He sends Nathan the Prophet to tell a story that mimics David's shame but with different details. When David is so outraged at the injustice of the perpetrator that he passes judgment on the man in absentia, Nathan reveals that the man is David himself, and the judgment of the Lord is upon him.

Nathan relays the Lord's curse upon him for his sin and flagrant disregard of the Lord of heaven as well as his violation of the law of Moses. The curse is two-fold and is revealed in chapter 12 verse 10 and following:

> Now therefore, the sword shall never depart from your house, because you have despised Me and have taken the wife of Uriah the Hittite to be your wife. Thus says the LORD, "Behold, I will raise up evil against you from your own household; I will even take your wives before your eyes, and give them to your companion, and he shall lie with your wives in broad daylight. Indeed you did it secretly, but I will do this thing before all Israel, and under the sun." Then David said to Nathan, "I have sinned against the LORD." And Nathan said to David, "The LORD also has taken away your sin; you shall not die." (2 Samuel 12:10–13, NASB)

The baby that was born of that shameful union died shortly after birth. The curse manifested itself with the rape of Tamar, David's daughter by her half-brother Amnon and his subsequent murder by Absalom, their other brother.

Absalom developed such a hatred for David because of David's failure to do justice for Tamar that he attempted to overthrow David's rule, publicly humiliated David with David's own concubines and was killed for his rebellion while being hung by his long hair from a tree.

Sin always has terrible consequences but as can be seen in the example of David, the Lord's anointed King of Israel, adultery may carry some of the harshest. This is why the virtue of self-control (which is also a fruit of the Holy Spirit) must be practiced with the greatest fervor. Young adults are perhaps the most vulnerable as their passions are fueled by the strength, vigor, and intemperance of youth. The consequences to a young woman are life changing when she faces a teenage pregnancy. Not only for her but for those whose lives are tied to her. If she attempts the easy way out as David did, she risks her conscience and peace of mind for the rest of her life. Abortion is a horrible choice.

Perhaps the best way to avoid these horrible consequences is to avoid the situations that give them such influence over our lives. It may be that the Pharisees had the right idea but not the tools to avoid the greatest sin of all, pride. Even as Jesus said.

An Ounce of Prevention Is Worth a Pound of Cure

It always comes as a shock when it is suggested by older, experienced Christians that I am being too restrictive in my recommendations. When I go to a movie, is it something that I would invite the Lord along to see? This is not a legalistic search for self-righteousness but a heart-felt attempt to avoid temptations. It's not for the purpose of bragging rights to friends or fellow Christians about my piety but a sincere desire to be Christlike. When I was young, I knew a young Christian lady whom I really wanted to date. She was kind and gentle and good-natured, not to mention, lovely. I asked her out more than once and she refused. I was so disappointed. Later, one of her best friends told me that it wasn't personal. She just refused to allow herself to be tempted to sidetrack the plans that God had for her until she had finished college and went on to the vocation God had called her to. She felt certain that at that time God would send her a husband of His choosing. I was thoroughly impressed with her faith and her resulting self-discipline. I then resigned myself to the fact that it probably would not be me.

We should always respect our elders by fervently listening to the advice that they give, but in the end, we must each one give account to Lord for our actions (2 Corinthians 5:9ff.) I am sure she was matched with many godly young men by concerned parents, hers and theirs, but the decision and consequences were hers.

• CHAPTER •
11

PERSEVERANCE

> And we desire that each one of you show the same diligence to the full assurance of hope until the end, [12]that you do not become sluggish, but imitate those who through faith and patience inherit the promises.
> —Hebrews 6:11–12, NKJV

In the last chapter, I spoke of a young woman who made a difficult social choice for the sake of her devotion to the Lord. In her devotion, she had to practice self-discipline to keep the promises she had made to the Lord and to herself. But there was more involved than momentary self-control. She had to continuously say "No" particularly since she was persistently sought by young men.

This continued self-discipline is another virtue, perseverance. Self-discipline over a lifetime is perseverance. Perseverance is continuing on the path of discipleship particularly in the face of persecution and suffering. It means endurance. It is easy to say "No" when everyone whom you respect supports you; it's quite another when they think you are wrong or disrespectful or selfish or even foolish.

Our Perseverance as a Reflection of His Perseverance

Perseverance is not only described as a virtue, but it is also a theological position. It is a position held by John Calvin and Reformed theologians to describe the continued and eternal salvation of the born-again Christian. It has in mind the continued and ever-faithful grace the Lord has for His children. It never fails or falters. It is dependable and trustworthy. If the Lord says a thing, it is true and will always be. This truly is His perseverance. When God commands or exhorts us to action, He expects us to carry it through to completion, and that is ours. Our perseverance is merely a reflection of His perseverance.

We tend to think of perseverance from the perspective of the Christian or essentially of our own, especially since it is primarily used in association with patient endurance of suffering, like a soldier enduring the pain of his wound. But the term also indicates the enduring of the judgment of other men's sins by the Lord on His cross. "Looking unto Jesus, the author and finisher of our faith, who for the joy that was set before Him endured the cross, despising the shame, and has sat down at the right hand of the throne of God" (Hebrews 12:2, NKJV).

The effectiveness of His sacrifice perseveres because it occurred once and was sufficient forever. Further, perseverance means to continue believing and enduring and working in the face of persecution and suffering.

We can never begin to understand His suffering on the cross for us because we have no understanding about the depth of God's repugnance at not just the sin of one individual but the cumulative sin of every soul who has ever lived or will live and the indescribable suffering that innocent ones have suffered because of it. The justice of God must have been so outraged that the fires of hell could never be hot enough. And all of that anger would have been directed toward Jesus on the cross for my sake. And because He was innocent and death had no hold on Him, it must have been endless and beyond understanding to the mortal mind how it could have been willingly endured. Death would not be a release.

At any moment, Jesus could have shaken off the suffering, called myriads of angels, stepped down off the cross and no longer endured it. The suffering that took all time for humans to create could have ended in a few moments. But the consequences for us would have been devastating. We would still be in our sin awaiting rightful judgment. But Jesus loved us so much that He was willing to endure it or persevere in His unjust suffering because of us. Our perseverance in suffering has no value at all in comparison.

Christian Examples of Perseverance

Certainly, human suffering could never be compared to the Lord's on the cross on our behalf, but the suffering of others can certainly be compared to mine personally and therefore, show me the depth of perseverance of my martyred brothers and sisters.

Hebrews chapter 11 is sometimes referred to as the "faith chapter." It can also be thought of in terms of patient endurance by those great men and women of God who have suffered for their faith in the past, even to a martyr's death. The writer reveals a large list of many of the greatest warriors of the faith and what they endured and how they persevered. Yet we are certain that the list is in no way complete. Throughout history the list of those who endured persecution and suffering for the cause of Christ has provided numerous books and sermons. Undoubtedly, this is why the Lord provided them for us.

Being Christian means that we live as Christ lived. Every breath we take becomes a testimony to the goodness of God's grace and to His never-failing presence. Our life as ambassadors for the Kingdom of Heaven is reflected to the world in our daily willingness to walk in faith. It doesn't mean in sinless perfection but in constant devotion to our commitment to the Lord and our thankfulness and faithfulness towards Him.

The true test of our salvation is perseverance. Jesus said in Mathew 10:22 and 24:14, "He who endures to the end will be saved." It's easy to just drop back and let someone else run the race but Hebrews gives us a warning in chapter 2:

Therefore we must give the more earnest heed to the things we have heard, lest we drift away. For if the word spoken through angels proved steadfast, and every transgression and disobedience received a just reward, how shall we escape if we neglect so great a salvation, which at the first began to be spoken by the Lord, and was confirmed to us by those who heard Him. (Hebrews 2:1–3, NKJV)

The term for *drift* is like a piece of wood in a lazy stream just floating along with the current. It indicates a lack of resistance and a willingness to be moved along by the power of something else. Of course, we know that if we let go, sin will drive us to complacency and apathy. The Lord called it "lukewarm," and He said He would vomit us out (Revelation 3:16). This passage is directed at an entire church, the church at Laodicea. It does not mean that Jesus will abandon His children. It does show us the need for Christians to stay diligent and stick to the Way. I am sure that not all the Laodiceans were slack, but I am also sure that those who weren't had to leave or suffer the fate of those who didn't. Hebrews has five warnings against falling back. John tells us in the Revelation regarding the

Laodicean Church, "As many as I love, I rebuke and chasten. Therefore be zealous and repent" (Revelation 3:19, NKJV).

Unlike Solomon, our lives should reflect our belief in God's eternal love for us. King Solomon is one of the most famous apostates in human history. Maybe it is because he was so blessed of the Lord with wisdom and success that his turning away seems more tragic than most.

Perhaps Paul is the greatest example of perseverance short of Jesus Himself. The New Testament is replete with examples of Paul's unerring perseverance both intentionally delineated and unintentional. In 2 Corinthians 16:26–33, Paul gives a litany of sufferings that he endured for the cause of Christ. An amazing list of torments and hardships endured that would have surely turned the most deliberate of Christians back. Nothing but the boundless grace of God could allow such temptation to be endured.

The good news is that we do not have to face the world and its barriers alone. We have the promised Holy Spirit who helps us and gives us the power to resist. We need not live in defeat. We can be forgiven and reinstated just as if nothing happened. The wonderful "hang in there, baby" is 1 John 1:9, "If we confess our sins, He is faithful and just to forgive us our sins and to cleanse us from all unrighteousness" (NKJV).

We also have each other. Every one of us has known the experience of the defeat, guilt, and shame of sin. We all have suffered with sin in our Christian lives. We can find comfort and assurance in the forgiveness of sin from our Lord and encouragement and support from those in our local church. That is supposed to be one of the great benefits of regular church membership. I know that it's not always the case, but as we learned earlier, if we do not forgive others, God will not forgive us. Rest assured, the Lord will deal with those people. Just remember that the Lord perseveres in His promises and never ever fails.

The chapter of faith is a memorial to the perseverance of the faithful. It is a wall of remembrance. An honor roll for the greatest and best of us. And finally, it is a goal line to be reached and crossed for those who would hear, "Well done thou good and faithful servant."

• CHAPTER •
12

Godliness

> And without controversy great is the mystery of godliness: God was manifested in the flesh, Justified in the Spirit, Seen by angels, Preached among the Gentiles, Believed on in the world, Received up in glory.
> —1 Tim 3:16, NKJV

"As important and intriguing as divine depths might be, they defy discovery by the natural means of our minds. He reserves these things for those whose hearts are completely His . . . for those who take the time to wait before Him. Only in that way can there be intimacy with the Almighty."[30] Swindoll describes his passion for the Father, and it could be that this is what godliness is.

Godliness is probably the most enigmatic of all the virtues. The reason is because it is not specifically defined in Scripture. The Greek word translated "godliness" is

---
[30] Swindoll, *Intimacy with the Almighty*. 15.

εὐσέβεια. It is generally defined as "piety." That's kind of like saying "cosmos" describes the universe. No one would deny that godliness can be defined with one word. But for understanding, it just doesn't do the trick. Kind of like a cucumber sandwich when you're really hungry.

Godliness is the desire to cooperate with God the Heavenly Father in every way possible. It is cooperation with our understanding of His plan and with our understanding of who He is (His nature and character). As Jerry Bridges notes in his book, "Godliness is more than Christian Character. Its character that springs from devotion to God."[31] Godliness is what being "born again" leads us to be when we surrender ourselves to Him. It is the manifestation of the spiritual change brought on by the working of the indwelling of Holy Spirit.

Good works are evidence of the new life. Paul says it, "Therefore, my beloved, as you have always obeyed, not as in my presence only, but now much more in my absence, work out your own salvation with fear and trembling" (Philippians 2:12, NKJV). Obedience is certainly part of it, but fear of punishment will not motivate us to intimacy, however, devotion will. Paul is talking about reverence not terror. When we operate from love and devotion, our works are indicative of our attitude. Godliness is indicative of a

---

[31.] Jerry Bridges, *The Pursuit of Holiness ; The Pursuit of Holiness: Bible Study ; The Practice of Godliness* (Colorado Springs, Colo.: NavPress, 2001). *The Practice of Godliness. 15.*

maturing Christian's desire to please our Heavenly Father. In this sense, the baby Christian has it on much older and "mature" Christians. Godliness is a passion for intimacy with the Father and His Son Jesus.

Godliness is one of the most difficult virtues to quantify because it is so subjective. Just as our salvation is personal and our response to the Lord's call is also personal, our Christian walk also is very personal.

Godliness is wanting to know God, and this can only be accomplished by knowing His Son. Jesus is the only means to the Father. "Jesus said to him, "I am the way, the truth, and the life. No one comes to the Father except through Me" (John 14:6, NKJV).

Godliness is Devotion to God

A relationship with God requires humility because God hates pride. "The fear of the Lord is to hate evil; Pride and arrogance and the evil way And the perverse mouth I hate" (Proverbs 8:13, NKJV). One of the hardest things to do for a proud person is to be still and listen. We always feel like our opinions are significant. Not true when we pray. We bow our heads (an act of humility), and we listen. When I quietly listen, I hear no audible voice, but I know peace. It flows through me like a quiet stream, and it brings joy. Such peace is more effective than any sedative. It is from joy that I can praise and worship my Savior. And as I quietly listen, the Lord shows me my direction.

Praise and worship to me are the essence of devotion. John tells us, "But the hour is coming, and now is, when the true worshipers will worship the Father in spirit and truth; for the Father is seeking such to worship Him" (John 4:23, NKJV). When Elijah prayed from the mountaintop, the Lord's presence went by, and the wind roared and broke apart the rocks followed by an earthquake and a fire, but the Lord did not speak from those. He spoke with a small, delicate voice (1 Kings 19:12 ff). The Psalmist relays the message from God, "Be still, and know that I am God; I will be exalted among the nations, I will be exalted in the earth!" (Psalm 46:10, NKJV).

When I sit in a quiet place, I pray and ask the Lord to open my heart and mind granting me understanding and wisdom. I then open His word and begin to read expecting to receive enlightenment from Him. He never fails. It is in these quiet times that I find peace and strength to do my daily necessities. I begin with joy, peace, and wisdom. These are tools that bring me through the day and leave me thankful and blessed at the end of day. It doesn't always work out that way. Especially when adversity and confrontation and attacks by the enemy distract me, it seems that God is not near. It is a lie. He is always there with love and grace. That is my devotion, and all anyone has to do is believe and wait on the Lord.

The Enemy of Godliness

But being part of Peter's list of progressive virtues that lead to authentic spiritual maturity, we know that godliness is something that we, ourselves, can practice and improve upon. There is, however, a hindrance to our progress. It is the same thing that hinders every aspect of our spiritual growth. It's how the enemy distracts us throughout our day, stealing our joy and our peace.

Every Christian is an individual because each of us has a carnal nature that seeks its own satisfaction rather than the will of the Lord. Each is unique in response to carnality, but the goal of being Christlike is to let the world see Jesus through us. As Paul says, "I have been crucified with Christ; it is no longer I who live, but Christ lives in me; and the life which I now live in the flesh I live by faith in the Son of God, who loved me and gave Himself for me" (Galatians 2:20, NKJV). And when either death releases us or the Lord returns, we live to be fully glorified in that we die being like Him.

"Beloved, now we are children of God; and it has not yet been revealed what we shall be, but we know that when He is revealed, we shall be like Him, for we shall see Him as He is" (1 John 3:2, NKJV). This is a source of hope to me. I know that at the end of this journey, I will drop this old nature, and I will be changed into His likeness. I will no longer fight selfishness but will know death to be swallowed up into His victory.

But each of us battles his own flesh in very individual ways. In essence, selfishness is the enemy of godliness. We place ourselves on the throne of our wills, and that is contrary to godliness which is all about placing the Lord Jesus there.

That will naturally result in concentrations in certain areas of our spiritual walk over other areas. Men and women will be different as well as adults and young people. Without doubt, the primary goal is to make us as Christlike as possible, but selfishness will always try to promote itself. The aim of Christian growth is to allow Christ to live through us.

Even when the apostles penned Scripture, they were not writing from themselves but were illuminated by the Holy Spirit "For prophecy never came by the will of man, but holy men of God spoke as they were moved by the Holy Spirit" (2 Peter 1:21, NKJV).

It is through the wondrous grace of our Lord that we have one of the biggest helps imaginable. Even though our battle is subjective and individual, we must realize that others have faced these sins and offer the Christian voice of experience. This help can be found in the church. It's why God commands us to seek out the local fellowship,

And let us consider one another in order to stir up love and good works, not forsaking the assembling of ourselves together, as is the manner of some, but exhorting one another, and so much the more as you see the Day approaching. (Hebrews 10:24–25, NKJV)

Godliness incorporates all the qualities of God's nature that can be manifested in man. It incorporates virtue, love, mercy, justice, selflessness, courage, righteousness, and sanctification just mentioning a few. Essentially, it is most of what makes a Christian human being different from a fleshly one that can be done by our own choices to be Christlike.

Examples of Godliness

One of the godliest men mentioned in Scripture is Daniel the Prophet. His faith is strong and unfailing from the moment of his captivity as a teen. He has the unusual and rare quality of being named "greatly beloved" by Gabriel the Archangel (Daniel 9:23, NKJV). The qualities of this man so "greatly beloved" are revealed in the book of Daniel from the first through the ninth chapters. It is there that we are introduced to Daniel, the man as well as Daniel the Prophet.

Daniel was carried away by King Nebuchadnezzar of Babylon in August 605 BC.[32] Daniel was probably carried off by Nebuchadnezzar in 605 BC just after his father Nabopolassar died. He rushed back to Babylon directly across the desert. He ordered Daniel and others to be carried back by a different route. In this particular time, many of the young, handsome, intelligent, and aristocratic men and women were carried back to Babylon to be trained as administrators and liaisons for the Jews.

Daniel was to be fed, clothed, educated, and supervised by Nebuchadnezzar's chief eunuch. In all of this, the goal was to alter Daniel's attitudes and belief system to encourage cooperation with the heathen Babylonians. His metamorphosis would need to destroy his faith in the LORD. They would destroy his will with moral defilement first by forcing him to accept special food and favors indicating collaboration.[33] But the primary aspect of godliness practiced by faithful people is courage and Daniel would have to say "No" in as inoffensive a way as possible. Not only would he have to resist but he would have to survive afterward. These people had complete control of his life and could execute him for no reason at all. In other words, passive resistance would be the path.

[32.] John Clement Whitcomb, *Daniel* (Chicago: Moody Press, 1985), 29.

[33.] Whitcomb. *Daniel* (1985), 30

Daniel not only survived as the conquered diplomat, he succeeded. Daniel was a faithful and courageous teen whose testimony was impressive enough to allow nonbelievers to see the greatness of the LORD. As an adult, Daniel was even faithful unto death in his prayer life. When a conspiracy to destroy him was concocted, he showed his persistence to godliness by praying in public when it was made illegal and carried the penalty of death. And not just death but death by starved lions. His courage was unfailing in his prayer life.

Godliness Versus Religion

Godliness requires courage, but religion only requires participation. Godliness is based on worship of the God of heaven, but religion can be about man with no reference to deity at all. Godliness is created by association with God, but religion can be a strictly man-made endeavor.

Jeremiah had delivered the Word of God to Jerusalem in Jeremiah 29 and following telling Jerusalem and King Zedekiah to accept the captivity of Babylon and pray for its peace and so they of the captivity would have peace in the land God had sent them to. He told them that seventy years' banishment from the land would end, and God would bring them back home. Even in the midst of suffering from God's righteous judgments, the people would know peace. He would even speak to them through prophets that He would send in their place of banishment, judgment, and suffering. Even so God does not abandon His people. Of course, Daniel would be greatest among them. We have already seen that godliness was a quality of Daniel the Prophet.

What a marvelous God is ours! With such a loving God, our devotions, our worship, and our praise should not stop. Our godliness should never falter, and as a function of our conversion, our godliness, which is manifested as courage, carry us through. When the world tells us to "conform, conform," it is our godliness that tells us to resist and prepare to counter with the Gospel.

In all the virtues, we have seen the working of Holy Spirit in our growth. It is no surprise that He also aids our spiritual growth in this virtue as well. But we ourselves have a big say about what form our godliness takes. Remember that all of these virtues are a command to us to "add to our faith." We then have to search out the aspects of our Christian walk which encourage and feed us through our daily lives as we move through our growth process. We are regular attenders at our local church of choice. We may dress up in our finest as an act of worship. We pray and tithe because it is a source of fulfillment and joy to do the things that the Lord has commanded of us. We teach Sunday school and heartily sing in the choir and in the congregation. We smile and greet one another because, strangely enough, we are truly glad to see brothers and sisters in Christ. We serve each other because God the Holy Spirit urges us to and rewards us for our ministry of worship. It is good to be a child of God and good to serve Him in purity, holiness, consecration, and love. We hear the prayer requests and praises for God's providence. We listen closely to the sermon as the messenger delivers God's encouragement, love, chastening, and warning to us. And in all of this, we know that God is with us and for us.

Godliness is an expression of our love for Him and is a way that we can be "proactive" and ingenious in our service and worship. It is where we can make our Christianity an effect of our devotion.

• C H A P T E R •
13

Brotherly Kindness

> Be kindly affectionate to one another with brotherly
> love, in honor giving preference to one another.
> —Romans 12:10, NKJV

Sometimes a dictionary definition just doesn't seem to do the job. In order to understand a term, many times, we have to compare it to other terms. "Brotherly love/kindness" may be one of those terms. "Love" is definitely one of those terms. At the beginning, I explained how love means different things to different people based on personal, subjective experiences. The understanding dissolves into "what it means to me." This thinking has been the bane of modern Christianity. For this reason, we will look at Scripture and life experiences for examples of word definitions to eliminate the emotional responses and influences. In order to do this, it is necessary to understand what Peter meant by "brotherly love/kindness." After all, he had a discussion with the Lord after His resurrection involving this very subject. John 21:15–19 reveals this conversation. (Inserted are the original language words for "love.")

> So when they had eaten breakfast, Jesus said to Simon Peter, "Simon, son of Jonah, do you love (ἀγαπάω) Me more than these?" He said to Him, "Yes, Lord; You know that I love (φιλέω the verbal form of φιλαδελφία) You." He said to him, "Feed My lambs." He said to him again a second time, "Simon, son of Jonah, do you love (ἀγαπάω) Me?" He said to Him, "Yes, Lord; You know that I love (φιλέω) You." He said to him, "Tend My sheep." He said to him the third time, "Simon, son of Jonah, do you love (φιλέω) Me?" Peter was grieved because He said to him the third time, "Do you love (φιλέω) Me?" And he said to Him, "Lord, You know all things; You know that I love (φιλέω) You." Jesus said to him, "Feed My sheep. Most assuredly, I say to you, when you were younger, you girded yourself and walked where you wished; but when you are old, you will stretch out your hands, and another will gird you and carry you

where you do not wish." This He spoke, signifying by what death he would glorify God. And when He had spoken this, He said to him, "Follow Me." (John 21:15–19, NKJV)

The original words actually follow the correct Greek grammar of the text in their proper tense, voice, and mood conventions for verbs, but for our purposes, the root verbal form is sufficient. Notice that Jesus acknowledges the difference in the two words by using Peter's word in the third repetition.

Peter is distressed because the Lord repeated the same question three times. At this point, we know from what we read in Acts that Peter is uneducated and may not know the nuance of what the Lord is saying, but we do. He is clearly showing a difference between the words with ἀγάπη (pronounced *agape*) being the more spiritually significant of the two.

The word that Peter uses for brotherly kindness in 2 Peter is φιλαδελφία (pronounced *philadelphia*). It is clear that he knows the difference at this point (at the writing of 2 Peter) since he shows ἀγάπη as a virtue advanced upon φιλαδελφία in spiritual development and as the next step in the progression.

The word is composed of two parts. The first part is φιλέω or *phile'w* which means "I love" and the second which is ἀδελφός or *adelphos* meaning "brother." In the Greek of Peter's circle, the word meant love or affection for someone in your church group, but earlier in ancient Greek it meant, love for close friends, comrades, or family, love of brothers and sisters. Literally, it means love for someone in your circle of friends and family to the ancient Greeks.

As is often the case, the world has a different idea about meanings from Christians. Many times, the world associates heroism and extraordinary actions with the word "love." An example is patriotism or love of country. But, as extraordinary as the word is, it is expected every moment from the Lord's people.

In English, one word describes "love," but in Greek as many as six words carry the understanding. We will deal with only two for now. The first, of course, is φιλαδελφία, and it is the one that Peter uses, but the second word is ἀγάπη, the one that Jesus uses in John 21. Jesus defined this word in the Sermon on the Mount. He said, "But I say to you who hear: Love your enemies, do good to those who hate you, bless those who curse you, and pray for those who spitefully use you" (Luke 6:27–28, NKJV). The word He uses here is ἀγαπάω (pronounced *agapao*) which is the verbal form of ἀγάπη. It means "love" as an action.

Definitions are great and they clue us into the culture and thinking of the person who uses the word, but there is much more to most words than just concise definitions.

Paul's Account of Brotherly Love

There is an account of brotherly love and filial obligation in the New Testament. It is written by Paul and relates the incidence of an escaped slave named Onesimus. The account is the letter to Philemon.

Many people just skip over it and say it's just a personal correspondence between Paul and an old friend, but Holy Spirit put it in the canon for a reason. It is a marvelous example of Christian brothers, who are not related by parentage, and a situation that exists between them involving another unrelated Christian brother.

To begin with, Philemon is a book about forgiveness. As Merrill C. Tenney writes, "It is a practical lesson in the petition of the prayer, 'Forgive us our debts as we forgive our debtors.'"[34] Paul's greeting is addressed to the entire church, several individuals and not just Philemon. But Philemon is specifically mentioned in the salutation, in his own sentence at the beginning, and as we read on, we realize this is a personal letter to be witnessed by the entire church. The letter is not just an example of Paul's affection for the church and Philemon in particular but of Onesimus as well. But there is more to it.

---

[34] Merrill C. Tenney and Walter M. Dunnett, *New Testament Survey*, Rev (Grand Rapids, Mich. : Leicester, England: W.B. Eerdmans Pub. Co. ; Inter-Varsity Press, 1985), 319.

In their Introduction to the New Testament, Carson, Moo, and Morris state, "On the basis of love, Paul appeals for Onesimus, whom he calls 'my son' adding 'who became my son while I was in chains,'" (8–10).[35] Paul states his confidence in Philemon's love because of the reports of others and makes his appeal for Onesimus based on it. So, in essence, it is regarding Philemon's loving reputation and as a brother in Christ that Paul makes his request. Apparently, Onesimus was a runaway slave who not only did not return but robbed Philemon as well. But, having escaped, he ran into Paul and was converted. Paul shows great love for Onesimus, whom he probably doesn't know well in a worldly way, by offering to pay off his debt to Philemon and begging him to forgive his former slave. His appeal is very emotional, and he even resorts to reminding Philemon of his own past debt to Paul. Such love is very deep and extraordinary. Many would not assume such a debt for an unrelated brother, yet this is what Christian "brotherly love" is. Onesimus was a thief, a criminal, and an evil person who took advantage of Philemon and his loving nature. Anyone who has been a victim of such a relationship is well aware of the feelings it leaves behind. The enemy takes great joy in such betrayal. Paul with his "tough love" not only helps Onesimus on the right path like Christ and

---

[35] D. A. Carson, Douglas J. Moo, and Leon Morris, *An Introduction to the New Testament*, New Testament Studies (Grand Rapids, Mich: Zondervan, 1992), 387.

Zacchaeus (Luke 19:2ff) but helps Philemon not develop a root of bitterness, and in addition, the church sees a beautiful example of restoration and loving forgiveness.

The love we share for each other as a church is a familial love in the bond of Jesus Christ and our common salvation. Many people grew up in church hearing our dads referred to by others as "brother" and our moms as "sister." Even today many call each other by such familiar names because of their common bond. Yet the familial love shared by those in the church is much more intimate because of the presence of Holy Spirit uniting us together in the "Spirit of Love." "The Spirit Himself bears witness with our spirit that we are children of God" (Romans 8:16, NKJV). In this is the uniqueness of brotherly love amongst Christians.

Many times, I have said that the world can always find "buddies" and "booze" at the bars, but real brothers and sisters can only be found in God's church. People need other people to love and to be loved by. We need security, intimacy, and peace. Buddies can be found on the sunny side, but when the rain comes, where are they? Sounds like a country western song, doesn't it?

Crippled Love

Love doesn't come easy. Spiritual growth requires effort and consistency. Not everyone in the church has the desire to be a "brother" or a "sister." Bitterness and unforgiveness destroy joy and separate us from God's blessings. We can become the angry and sad old curmudgeons that everyone recalls from our early church experiences. We must care for each other and forgive each other as if each of us was a family member.

Every Christian can recall being used, unacknowledged, forgotten, or disregarded. Many people, even Christians, wear their feelings on their sleeves, walking around expecting to be slighted. They're like prize fighters dancing around the ring ready for action. Such people are their own unhappiness. Others look past human frailties, remembering their own inadequacies. The older Christians grow thick skins and give God the glory, which is His right. They pray and forgive. Most know what the "root of bitterness" is, and why it is much more profitable to avoid it rather than to be self-righteous. Many Christians live miserable lives because they press their "rights," failing to forgive when "wronged." They become unhappy prize fighters. The Lord tells us when we pray we must forgive; else, He will not forgive us. Forgiveness allows us to put bad and carnal things behind us. It allows us joyful worship together without guilt and shame. This fellowship is one of the sustaining things for Christians in times of persecution and conflict.

The sanctuary we seek is not only physical but spiritual and psychological as well. Knowing that on Sunday and at other times together, we can receive sanctuary from our Christian family. It has been a blessing from the Lord that has sustained me. Yes, there are always those who see themselves as the primary focus and the center of attention. Grudging cooperation can rarely be hidden. Most people can sense the hard feelings in others, and it causes difficulties. But most of us understand that when love and acceptance are expressed, everyone is strengthened. Paul tells us,

> Therefore if there is any consolation in Christ, if any comfort of love, if any fellowship of the Spirit, if any affection and mercy, fulfill my joy by being like-minded, having the same love, being of one accord, of one mind. Let nothing be done through selfish ambition or conceit, but in lowliness of mind let each esteem others better than himself. Let each of you look out not only for his own interests, but also for the interests of others. (Philippians 2:1–4, NKJV)

This is Paul's formula for peace in the church. He goes on to tell us that it was the Lord's example to humble Himself even though He was then and is now the Lord of heaven and earth. If our Lord can do this for us, surely, we can do this for each other. Jesus teaches this very lesson to His disciples,

> So when He had washed their feet, taken His garments, and sat down again, He said

> to them, "Do you know what I have done to you? You call Me Teacher and Lord, and you say well, for so I am. If I then, your Lord and Teacher, have washed your feet, you also ought to wash one another's feet. For I have given you an example, that you should do as I have done to you. Most assuredly, I say to you, a servant is not greater than his master; nor is he who is sent greater than he who sent him. If you know these things, blessed are you if you do them. (John 13:12–17, NKJV)

The lesson of the foot washing is humble service to one another—seeking each other's greater good and, not ourselves, counting others more highly than ourselves. Spiritual growth in many Christians, even mature ones, stops there.

Unless the self is put aside and dethroned from the place of authority in our lives, we will never be able to serve the Lord effectively. As long as we harbor unforgiveness, bitterness, and resentment, we unseat the Lord and place our own desires on the throne of our wills. We condemn ourselves to a miserable life of "shoulda, coulda, woulda." In other words, a sad existence of regret and self-recrimination. How can we love others if we cannot even love ourselves? The answer is, "We can't."

• CHAPTER •
14

Divine Love

You have heard that it was said, "You shall love your neighbor and hate your enemy." But I say to you, love your enemies, bless those who curse you, do good to those who hate you, and pray for those who spitefully use you and persecute you, that you may be sons of your Father in heaven; for He makes His sun rise on the evil and on the good, and sends rain on the just and on the unjust. For if you love those who love you, what reward have you? Do not even the tax collectors do the same? And if you greet your brethren only, what do you do more than others?

Do not even the tax collectors do so? Therefore, you shall be perfect, just as your Father in heaven is perfect.

—(Matthew 5:43–48, NKJV)

With these verses, we can see a great difference between "brotherly love" and "Divine Love." It is a difference that Peter should have recognized since this message was delivered early in the Lord's Galilean ministry during His Sermon on the Mount. Even Peter had to grow.

The Lord tells us that we must love not only family and friends but our enemies as well. This is an action requiring divine empowerment since none can love with such purity by their own ability. It is a great affirmation of God's overwhelming power in the lives of Christians that such a thing can be commanded with any expectation of success. Yet Jesus does exactly this. In war, soldiers invariably love their immediate brothers in arms and their countries.

Almost all of the Medal of Honor winners, who have been interviewed, have borne witness that their great deeds were driven by concern for those same brothers in arms who were in imminent danger. But to command these men to die for the very ones who are threatening their brothers is unimaginable, yet such is what the Lord says.

Of all the virtues previously discussed, we can deceive ourselves that we are sincere. But this one is impossible to counterfeit. Proof requires the death of the participant. Paul says, "I have been crucified with Christ; it is no longer I who live, but Christ lives in me; and the life which I now live in the flesh I live by faith in the Son of God, who loved me and gave Himself for me" (Galatians 2:20, NKJV).

This love is the love that sent Jesus to the cross for the sake of the Roman soldier who drove the spear into His side. And even those who unjustly sentenced Him to death "for the good of the nation" as He uttered, "Father, forgive them."

Αγάπη, Divine Love of God the Father

While upon this Earth, we will never understand the love of God that will take enemies and adopt them as sons and daughters; that will make them kings and priests in His heavenly kingdom.

The only way is to take what the Scripture says regarding His divine love and highlight it in terms of grace, forgiveness, redemption, restoration, mercy, and holiness. As Abraham raised his hand to slaughter Isaac, the Lord stayed him.

God's love for us surpasses our human understanding. We don't even know what to think of it, but that is what God the Father did on our behalf with His Son, Jesus.

John describes God's nature in his first epistle as "Love." As Palmer states, "Or to put it another way, love springs forth from the character of God himself."[36] This led Him to make the unthinkable sacrifice on our behalf. John 3:16 says, "For God so loved the world that He gave His only begotten Son, that whoever believes in Him should not perish but have everlasting life" (John 3:16, NKJV). That is to say that the overwhelming characteristic of our Heavenly Father is a quality containing all the things that we as guilty trespassers could hope for in our Judge. He loves us. But He loved His Son as well. It was unjust for

---

[36.] Earl F. Palmer, *Love Has Its Reasons: An Inquiry into New Testament Love* (Waco, Tex: Word Books, 1977), 23.

Him to die because He had done no wrong. One thing is certain that God knew that His Only Born Son would not stay in that tomb for long. That when the work of atonement was finished, the Lord Christ would come out of the tomb, bodily alive and hungry.

Our salvation is a direct result of God's love for us. Essentially, all the qualities previously mentioned are incorporated in salvation and provided by His love.

Love, the Only Gift That We Can Give to God

We who love the Lord and wonder how we can serve Him find ourselves in the old Christmas-time dilemma, "What to give to the man who has everything?" What can we give to God that He doesn't already own? How about our new hearts? Heart is a euphemism for the seat of emotions. That emotion to God must be love—the same kind that He has for us. Everything that is precious to Him stems from love, our devotion, our service, our worship, our giving, our gifts, and the list goes on. God doesn't demand our love, but He desires it. The key to giving our love is devotion. We can give Him our love in our devotion.

Divine love is the basis of all that we as Christians do to accomplish the Great Commission. It is the engine of Christian ministry. Ministry requires us to step out of our comfort zones and into a world that crucified our Savior. Divine love is the only force strong enough to induce in our hearts missionary effort in places of depravation and want. William Carey labored for more than ten years, suffering the deaths of most of his family including his beloved wife before he saw conversions to Christianity. In my home church, ladies work tirelessly to decorate for special occasions. They prepare our building for funerals, marriages, baby showers, and the list goes on. All for no reward except the joy of serving their Savior's people. It is the calling of every Christian.

The Supremacy of Love for Ministry

No discussion about the love of God is complete without including a close look at 1 Corinthians 13. It is the unequivocal masterpiece on the subject. Written by the Apostle Paul but inspired by the Holy Spirit, it conveys the utter futility of the Christian experience without it.

Love is the essential part of the Christian walk; it is essential to all aspects of ministry. It is necessary because of the ineffectiveness of ministry to others in the power of our own will and ability. Without love, service is nothing more than self-gratification and a waste of time.

Love gives all ministry, no matter how bumbling, a sense of God's approval and proof that God is involved because it reflects His very nature. Our children tend to reflect us because of genetics and more importantly, upbringing. Just as certain qualities are apparent in our children, so the love of God should be apparent in us.

Paul begins his treatise with the assurance that all human endeavor in Christian experience is of no value if love is not an integral part of it. Knowledge without love is merely an academic exercise. Faith without love is not pleasing to God. Asceticism or self-denial is just suffering without any redeeming purpose. Even martyrdom serves no purpose without love.

Paul continues his theme by explaining the qualities of love that make Christian ministry so effective. He describes first of all the characteristics of love that aid the Christian doing ministry. Love works inside the heart of the Christian to change it. This is how anyone becomes a minister (not just a pastor but anyone who proclaims Christ).

The minister finds patience where before there was little or no tolerance. Ministering Christians react to adversity and confrontation gently while explaining the Gospel to an argumentative seeker. They are not self-serving egoists nor are they jealous of other's successes. As Paul teaches, "Some indeed preach Christ even from envy and strife, and some also from goodwill" (Philippians 1:15, NKJV).

The minister is polite and not offensive in relations with other people even though the Gospel itself may offend an unrepentant sinner or backslidden Christian. The mature Christian is not a schemer or a manipulator. He takes people at face value until they prove otherwise. Such a person endures and even suffers loss for the Gospel's sake.

The mature Christian loves to see justice done and hates seeing evil succeed. It brings joy when the truth comes out. The loving Christian holds the tongue and doesn't speak ill of others. The quality of long-suffering endurance is a hallmark. Loving Christians are a source of confidence in the final outcome and hope for the future.

The greatest test of anything is its staying power. "He who laughs last laughs best" is a familiar quote which shows us that nothing is greater than the eternal. If something never fails, it is perfect. Love can be depended on to reveal to us all the things which God intends for us, and it never fails to accomplish its task. Love is eternal.

When Divine Love is Imitated

In 1 Corinthians, Paul teaches of the miraculous spiritual gifts bestowed upon the church by the Holy Spirit. But the Corinthians abused the gifts and turned them into a source of pride and elitism. Paul scolded them severely and taught them about true spirituality. He told them that Divine love is the only true indication that they are God's people. H. A. Ironside says, "The Divine Love is not something that is pumped up out of the natural heart; it is divinely given."[37]

In the time of the Corinthians, the pagans who worshipped in the temple of Dianna spoke in other-worldly "tongues." Of course, the obvious conclusion is that these supernatural gifts can all be counterfeited but divine love cannot.

Love is eternal, sufficient, and complete. Paul is saying to the Corinthians that the manifestation of the Holy Spirit's gifts in them is tainted beyond utility. His chide of their repugnant behavior to poor brothers and sisters at the "Agape feasts" in chapter 11 shows their misunderstanding of Christianity. There were only a few whose prophecies, knowledge, and tongues were fully inspired by the Holy Spirit. Only a handful whose spiritual manifestations could be trusted. Only a few who could actually relay the Word of God. Some were saying "in the spirit" that Jesus was accursed! (1 Cor. 12:3).

There are three things that are eternal according to Paul, "And now abide faith, hope, love, these three; but the greatest of these is love" (1 Corinthians 13:13, NKJV). The greatest of these is love and is the quality that above all else reveals us to be Christians. Without it, ministry is worldly.

---

[37] Henry Allan Ironside, *Addresses on the First Epistle to the Corinthians* (Neptune, NJ: Loizeaux Bros., 1988), 414.

CONCLUSION

The goal of discipleship is to create a follower who is like his master. The master teaches, and the follower listens and applies what he has learned. The goal of Christian discipleship is no different. It calls for the decrease of self and the increase of Christ living His life through us. Peter reminds us, "For if these things are yours and abound, you will be neither barren nor unfruitful in the knowledge of our Lord Jesus Christ" (2 Peter 1:8, NKJV).

The point of 2 Peter 1:1–11 is to show us how to increase in the knowledge of Christ to be fruitful, to have confidence in our salvation, and to have a glorious entrance into heaven when our time comes to leave this earth. Richard DeHaan sums it up for us by writing,

> The Apostle was concerned that his readers live in keeping with the glory of their salvation. He wanted them to be genuine, not hypocritical or artificial. He challenged them to develop the Christian graces of faith, virtue, knowledge, self-control, patience, godliness, brotherly kindness,

and love (2 Peter 1:5–7). God had done His part in providing His people with full salvation; now they were to do their part by working it out through the development of these graces.[38]

As our knowledge of Christ grows so must our surrender of ourselves to Him. The more Christlike we are, the more effective we will be in our ministry. If 2 Peter 1:1–11 has relayed to us a process that culminates in Divine Love crowning our growth, and we know that God's nature is Divine Love, and we know that Jesus Christ is God in the Flesh; we must believe that the process forms us into the image of Christ. We further have to believe that if Christ increases in us we, like Paul, must die daily. "I affirm, by the boasting in you which I have in Christ Jesus our Lord, I die daily" (1 Corinthians 15:31, NKJV). In essence, Peter's message is that Christ is Love, and the more Divine Love is developed in our Christian walk, the more Christlike we will become.

The more we gain the knowledge of Jesus Christ, the more like Him we will be.

We also have the greatest benefit a person can have to aid us in our journey. We have the promised indwelling Holy Spirit. He teaches us what we need to know. He

---

[38]. Richard W DeHaan, *Studies in Second Peter* (Wheaton, Ill.: Victor Books, 1977), 135.

understands exactly where we are and makes intercession for us in matters that we cannot even voice. We trust that the Lord has sent us His Spirit to help. In all of our journey, Holy Spirit is right there with us. He never leaves us and streamlines Peter's process for our particular shortcomings.

As we grow, Holy Spirit leads us to revisit areas where we tend to be weak and helps us to strengthen and reinforce what we have already learned. In other words, our growth process never stops. As a matter of fact, if it ever does, we don't just level off. It is the nature of our flesh that we will fall back in the process if we stop resisting. The writer of Hebrews warns, "For though by this time you ought to be teachers, you have need again for someone to teach you the elementary principles of the oracles of God, and you have come to need milk and not solid food" (Hebrews 5:12, NASB). I have chosen the NASB because it gives us a clear idea of what happens. We don't just drop back, but we need to be retaught the fundamentals of the faith. Sin obviously creates ignorance. We forget because sin brings us into slavery and by blinding us even as it does the lost world. It is a consequence of our carnal nature.

It's true that if we take our hands off the rudder, we give up control to whatever forces are at work. Our natural carnality will always drive us to sin. That is the battle: to keep our eyes on Christ, stay in His word, pray, and be diligent in our growth.

BIBLIOGRAPHY

Anderson, Neil T. The Bondage Breaker. Updated and expanded. Eugene, Or: Harvest House, 2000.

Branscomb, B. Harvie, B. Harvie. The Message of Jesus. Nashville, Tenn.: Abingdon-Cokesbury, 1926.

Bridges, Jerry. The Pursuit of Holiness; The Pursuit of Holiness: Bible Study ; The Practice of Godliness. Colorado Springs, Colo.: NavPress, 2001.

Brown, Mike. Accessed March 3, 2018. "College Dropouts and Student Debt," LendEDU (blog), November 2, 2017, https://lendedu.com/blog/college-dropouts-student-loan-debt/.

Bruce, F. F. The Time Is Fulfilled: Five Aspects of the Fulfilment of the Old Testament in the New. The Moore College Lectures 1977. Grand Rapids: Eerdmans, 1978.

Cairns, Earle Edwin. Christianity through the Centuries: A History of the Christian Church. Rev. and enl. ed., 2d ed. Grand Rapids, MI: Zondervan Pub. House, 1981.

Carson, D. A., Douglas J. Moo, and Leon Morris. An Introduction to the New Testament. New Testament Studies. Grand Rapids, MI.: Zondervan, 1992.

Crabb, Larry. Understanding People: Deep Longings for Relationship. Grand Rapids, MI: Ministry Resources Library, 1987.

DeHaan, Richard W. Studies in Second Peter. Wheaton, Ill.: Victor Books, 1977.

Gaebelein, Frank E., ed. *The Expositor's Bible Commentary: With the New Internat. Version of the Holy Bible* in 12 Vol. 10: Romans - Galatians. 19. print. Grand Rapids, MI.: Regency Reference Library, 1976.

Hodge, Charles. Systematic Theology. Grand Rapids MI.: Eerdmans, Reprint 1993.

Ironside, Henry Allan. Addresses on the First Epistle to the Corinthians. Neptune, NJ: Loizeaux Bros., 1988.

Jeremiah, David P. Prayer: The Great Adventure. Sisters, Or.: Multnomah Publishers, 2004.

Kempis, Thomas A. The Imitation of Christ. Moody Paperback Edition 1984. Editor Paul M. Bechtel. Chicago: Moody Press, 1980.

Lewis, C. S. Mere Christianity: A Revised and Enlarged Edition, with a New Introduction, of the Three Books, The Case for Christianity, Christian Behaviour, and Beyond Personality. Macmillan paperbacks ed. New York: Macmillan Pub. Co, 1984.

"List of Mental Disorders." Wikipedia, January 8, 2018. https://en.wikipedia.org/w/index.php?title=List_of_mental_disorders&oldid=819292528.

MacArthur, John. The Wrath of God. Moody Press ed. John MacArthur's Bible Studies. Chicago: Moody Press, 1986.

McQuilkin, Robertson J. An Introduction to Biblical Ethics. Wheaton, Illinois: Tyndale House Publishers, 1989.

"Milgram Experiment." Wikipedia, December 30, 2017. https://en.wikipedia.org/w/index.php?title=Milgram_experiment&oldid=817773912.

Palmer, Earl F. Love Has Its Reasons: An Inquiry into New Testament Love. Waco, Tex: Word Books, 1977.

Stott, John R. Basic Christianity. 1st ed. Grand Rapids, MI.: Eerdmans, 1986.

Strobel, Lee. The Case for Faith: A Journalist Investigates the Toughest Objections to Christianity. Grand Rapids, Zondervan Publishing House, 2000.

Swindoll, Charles R. Intimacy with the Almighty: Encountering Christ in the Secret Places of Your Life. Nashville, Tenn.: J. Countryman, 1999.

——— Rise & Shine: A Wake-up Call. Portland, Or: Multnomah, 1989.

——- The Grace Awakening. Dallas: Word Pub, 1990.

Tenney, Merrill C., and Walter M. Dunnett. New Testament Survey. Rev. Grand Rapids, MI.: Leicester, England: W.B. Eerdmans Pub. Co. ; Inter-Varsity Press, 1985.

Thiessen, Henry Clarence, and Vernon D. Doerksen. Lectures in Systematic Theology. Rev. Grand Rapids: Eerdmans, 1979.

Whitcomb, John Clement. Daniel. Chicago: Moody Press, 1985.

Wilcox, Stephen. "Alcohol, Drugs and Crime." Accessed January 27, 2018. https://www.ncadd.org/about-addiction/alcohol-drugs-and-crime.

ABOUT THE AUTHOR

Martin gave his life to the Lord Jesus in 1962. He married his wife Judy to whom he has been married for thirty-two years. He has a son, a daughter, and four grandchildren. The Lord called him into ministry, and when called to his first pastorate, his home church ordained him to the Gospel Ministry where he ministered bi-vocationally. When his ministry was completed there, he attended Liberty University and Liberty Baptist Theological Seminary where he was awarded a BS in pastoral ministries and a master of divinity. He received the Award for Academic Excellence in the master of arts in religion program. He has been a pastor both full time and part time from then until now. He is currently the adult ministries director at his home church.

CPSIA information can be obtained
at www.ICGtesting.com
Printed in the USA
FFHW020034080119
50077664-54913FF